Why I Left

THE
MORMON
CHURCH
and
Came
Back

Why I Left

THE MORMON CHURCH *and* *Came* *Back*

HALEIGH EVERTS

CFI

An imprint of Cedar Fort, Inc.
Springville, Utah

ISBN 13: 978-1-4621-2178-6

Published by CFI, an imprint of Cedar Fort, Inc.
2373 W. 700 S., Springville, UT 84663
Distributed by Cedar Fort, Inc., www.cedarfort.com

LIBRARY OF CONGRESS CATALOGING-IN-PUBLICATION DATA

Names: Everts, Haleigh, 1993- author.
Title: Why I left the Mormon Church and came back / Haleigh Everts.
Description: Springville, Utah : CFI, an imprint of Cedar Fort, Inc., [2018]
 | Includes bibliographical references and index.
Identifiers: LCCN 2017060361 (print) | LCCN 2018001385 (ebook) | ISBN
 9781462128723 (epub, pdf, mobi) | ISBN 9781462121786 (perfect bound : alk.
 paper)
Subjects: LCSH: Everts, Haleigh, 1993- | Mormon women--Biography. | Faith. |
 LCGFT: Autobiographies.
Classification: LCC BX8695.E94 (ebook) | LCC BX8695.E94 A3 2018 (print) | DDC
 289.3092 [B] --dc23
LC record available at https://lccn.loc.gov/2017060361

Cover design by Shawnda T. Craig
Cover design © 2018 Cedar Fort, Inc.
Edited and typeset by McKell Parsons and Jessica Romrell

Printed in the United States of America

10 9 8 7 6 5 4 3 2 1

Printed on acid-free paper

For everyone who's ever faced heartbreak, questioned their worth, or had doubts about their faith.

Contents

Contents

Acknowledgments

Thank you to my perfect match, my sweet husband, CJ, for never judging me or holding my past against me. For teaching me so much about the gospel and being an amazing example of faith to me. For helping me bring our beautiful daughter into this world. And for giving me my happily forever after.

Thank you to Kati Holland, for spending hours upon hours helping me write this book and taking the cover photo. You are the best soul friend.

Thank you to Ashley LeBaron, for being a true friend and standing by my side through every miserable thing I've done and felt, and for bringing so many smiles to my face during extremely difficult times. For helping me figure out how to even begin writing this book. Also for loving One Direction with me.

Thank you to my parents for being imperfect, but always trying your best. You motivated me to become the person I am today, a wife and mother and woman I'm proud to be.

Thank you to every single follower and subscriber who supports me and sends thoughtful messages of encouragement. My prayers are always with you and I love you.

Introduction

"All my life, my heart has sought a thing I cannot name."

—*Hunter S. Thompson*[1]

No matter where we are in the world—regardless of race, gender, age, or circumstance—we are all searching for something. Everyone is looking for the answers to life's questions; Everyone is looking for love, for happiness, to feel whole, to feel important and valued, to feel like they're not alone.

I have all those things. Because of The Church of Jesus Christ of Latter-day Saints, I've learned the answers to life's questions. I've developed a relationship with my Father in Heaven and my Savior Jesus Christ. I know where I came from, how the earth was created, what my purpose on earth is, and where I'm going when I die (for the most part). I know that even if it seems like no one on earth cares about me or loves me, I have Heavenly Parents who understand and love me more than I can imagine. I know that to Them, I am precious and of more worth than I can comprehend. I know I am never alone because Jesus Christ felt *exactly* what I feel, and the Holy Ghost is always available to comfort and guide me. I know I am here on the earth to receive a body, to learn and grow through life's difficult experiences and

1

trials, to become a wife and mother, to help others, and to prepare to live one day with my earthly and Heavenly family forever. I know after this earthly life I can receive eternal joy with those I love. With knowledge comes power and responsibility, and knowing these answers gives me the responsibility to live the gospel and keep the commandments and my covenants—but sometimes that's easier said than done.

I didn't always have these answers. I questioned these things, as many people do. Even after I learned some of these answers, I still doubted if they were true. When opposition came, I let fear and doubt creep in. Sometimes while we're here on earth living through those difficult experiences and trials, it's hard to see the eternal perspective. It's hard to always have faith and put trust in someone we don't physically see. It's hard to see the light at the end of the tunnel when the tunnel seems to be so dark and so long.

After starting a YouTube channel, I've had the opportunity to communicate with people around the world, and I've been surprised at how many young Latter-day Saints are choosing to leave the Mormon church like I did. But in many ways, I can relate to how they feel. I know when questions remain unanswered or temptation seems too hard to resist, the seemingly easier option is to just leave. Sometimes the testimony and answers we do have don't feel like they're enough to keep us going. Questioning the truthfulness of the gospel and figuring out your testimony isn't a bad thing—in fact, it's how you grow your faith. This is why conversion is a never-ending, lifelong process. But even after you receive a witness or surety that this gospel is true, even after you get your questions answered, life's trials and temptations can creep in. Even when you're at your strongest, the adversary will try his hardest to break you down and take away your faith. I never imagined I'd choose to leave the Church, but we all have to receive our own witness of the gospel—and it often doesn't come until after the trial of our faith.

My story starts in upstate New York where I grew up and where the LDS Church is quite small. My family is not Mormon—only my mother has been baptized—but I don't have much of a relationship with her. I was baptized when I was fifteen. At first I didn't mind living in a home with a family who didn't share my same beliefs; it forced me to depend on myself, to have a testimony, and to stand up for my religion. But eventually being the only member of the Church in my family and friend group became very confusing for me (especially when I started dating someone who wasn't LDS). I spent many years puzzling over temples and why we needed them in order to be with our families forever, questioning how my non-LDS family could ever be together forever, and wondering why God would separate families if they didn't accept this gospel, why God's promises to me weren't coming true, and why I had to experience such difficult trials and pain. I know I'm not alone in these questions, concerns, and doubts. Even if you were raised in the gospel of Jesus Christ, you have to grow a testimony of your own—and with that growth comes a time when you have to question and ask for yourself if the gospel is true. Sometimes, surprisingly, the answer isn't an immediate "yes."

This is my story of the heartbreak I've faced, the doubts and questions I had about the Mormon church, why I left the Mormon church. But it's also the story of how I later received answers to those questions, grew my faith, finally got everything I ever wanted in life, learned who I am and how to love myself, and continued to act in faith as a member of The Church of Jesus Christ of Latter-day Saints.

NOTE

1. Hunter S. Strange, *Hell's Angels: A Strange and Terrible Saga* (New York: Random House, 1966)

By Fire and Water

*"Yea, I say unto you come and fear not, and lay aside
every sin, which easily doth beset you, which doth
bind you down to destruction, yea, come and go
forth, and show unto your God that ye are willing to
repent of your sins and enter into a covenant with
him to keep his commandments, and witness it unto
him this day by going into the waters of baptism.*

*"And whosoever doeth this, and keepeth the commandments
of God from thenceforth, the same will remember that
I say unto him, yea, he will remember that I have
said unto him, he shall have eternal life."*

—Alma 7:15–16

PRE-MORMON DAYS

I'm not raised in a traditional family. Both my parents were married to other people before they were married to each other, and they get a divorce when I'm seven. While they both have kids from their previous marriages, my half-siblings are so much older than I am (my mother was forty-five when I was born). Because of this, I'm basically an only child.

After my parents' divorce, I live with my mother for a few years. But my mother is a businesswoman, and she is very busy working and taking care of her elderly parents and doesn't spend much time with me. On top of that, I just don't get along very well with my mother. She's very academic and cares a lot about my schooling and grades, and she mostly teaches me academic subjects like math and English—nothing about life or the real world. Our relationship struggles because we don't have similar interests and never spend much quality time together. Because of our differences, I feel like my mother doesn't understand me and expects me to be something I'm not, something that just isn't in my nature. I can never live up to her expectations of perfect grades; we will never bond through shared interests. She likes weird music and isn't musically talented like me and my dad. Her personality is so different from mine and my dad's; it's no wonder their marriage didn't work out. I'm naturally a lot more like my dad—he's funny and silly and playful and makes time to play with me and do things I enjoy. He cares about his appearance and takes good care of our house. He loves sports, good music that we sing to together, and movies, and is so full of wisdom. He always gives me life lessons and teaches me something important. Even though I'm young, my dad always tries to prepare me for life as an adult. I respect him so much for that.

I guess it's no surprise that, after a few years of living with my mother, we decide it would be best for me to live with my dad full time. I love my dad and I always had the best time with him anyway, so I'm much happier at his house. And my dad has retired due to a back injury, so he's always waiting for me when I got home from school— unlike my mother, who isn't available as much due to her other obligations. Because of our relationship and the fact that he's available more often, it just makes more sense for me to live with him during the week and stay with my mother on the weekends.

Being the child of divorced parents has its challenges; both my parents have made mistakes, and they both tell me about the other's mistakes—the things the other person has done to hurt them, the flaws the other person has, etc. But the things they tell me don't sway my opinions. I know who they are and how I feel about them. Nothing my mother says could change my mind about my dad. I'll always respect him for the good he does, and I'm grateful for the way he raises me. Even though he's done hurtful things, I'm able to forgive him and love him. Likewise, nothing my dad says makes me think any worse of my mother. Although we have our differences, I know she has good intentions and tries her best.

While my family isn't traditional or perfect, I've always known that I want my own family someday. Even as a little girl, I'm so excited to be a wife and mother. I love my baby dolls and knock on my mother's door, pretending I'm her long-lost daughter with a baby of my own and that we need someone to help us. I love playing house and pretending to be a mom, and I know that I'm going to be the best mom ever one day. I don't want to get divorced or be married more than once; I don't want kids from different marriages; and I don't want to have kids only raised by one parent. I want to get married and stay married. I want to make the right choice the first time and be with someone who wants to have a lot of kids. I've always wished I had siblings closer to my own age to play with, and I want my own kids to have what I didn't. I envision my own future family entirely different from the one I grew up in.

The Mormons at the Door

One spring afternoon, not long after I moved in with my dad, I'm staying at my mother's house for the weekend. I remember playing a computer game when the doorbell rings. My mother emerges from the back of the house to answer the door, and standing there are two young men from The Church of Jesus Christ of Latter-day Saints, dressed in suits. They're missionaries, and they want to teach us about their religion. My mother eagerly accepts their invitation—apparently missionaries have knocked on her door before. My dad isn't religious at all, so she was never able to learn from the missionaries while she was married to him. But now that she's single, this is the first opportunity she's had to invite them in and learn about their beliefs. My mother was born in Ireland and was (of course) raised Catholic. Being Catholic was a huge part of her culture and her heritage—not just a religion. I guess parts of Catholicism didn't make sense to her, but she never went searching for a church or a religion that had answers until the opportunity presented itself at her doorstep.

At the missionaries' invitation, we attend stake conference, and afterward we go to a family's house for brunch. Everyone is so friendly and welcoming. After that first Sunday, my mother is hooked. Over the next few months, she takes the missionary discussions and meets with people from this church. As I stay with my dad during the school week, I don't participate in these discussions, but I do attend church with my mother when I'm with her over the weekends. Finally, on her fifty-fifth birthday, my mother is baptized as a Mormon.

Her family is furious when she decides to become a Mormon. It's difficult for her to make this huge life change at fifty-five, but I guess she feels she received clarity to the questions she had about the Catholic church. I'm not sure what her questions were or the answers she's received through the Mormon Church, but she seems happy. My dad thinks it's very odd for her to become a Mormon so suddenly, especially because she also decides to start going by a new nickname. It's like she's becoming a different person, with a new name and new friends and a new perspective. Part of her interest, I think, is the community of the Mormon Church; my mother had just left a job she'd had for years, so it is probably comforting to her to make new friends and feel like she has a new home. Also, Mormons seem to have picture-perfect families and be so happy, which I think my mother finds appealing. They're also very helpful and do lots of service, and I know my mother enjoys receiving their help with things, as she's a single woman and alone most of the time.

I'm only ten at the time, but I like all the nice people too—there are lots of kids to play with. I don't feel like I really fit in with them, but they're nice, and I don't have any siblings my age or neighborhood kids to play with, which is very lonely for me. Because I stay with my mother on weekends, I go where she goes, so I attend church with her every Sunday. To be honest, I don't really understand what anyone at church is talking about. They talk about unfamiliar stories in a book called the Book of Mormon, and Primary seems so babyish with its silly games and strange new songs. But I go along with it because it's nice to be around other kids.

After a few months, my mother sets up appointments for me to meet with the missionaries and take the discussions for myself. After meeting with the missionaries a few times and going to church consistently, they ask me if I'd like to be baptized too. My mother was baptized so quickly, but I had never even considered that I could be baptized too. But I like the things I learned from the missionaries and I like going to church. Before I had ever heard of the Church, I felt the way I imagine Superman felt—he wasn't like everyone else, but he knew he had a special purpose. When I learn about the spirit world, how I'm a child of God, and that I came to the earth for a purpose, I realize I was right the whole time. I *am* here for a special reason. I *am* different. I also really like the idea that I could be with my family forever. I think most people imagine their loved ones waiting for them when they die, but the Mormon Church actually teaches how that's possible. I think over all these things I like about the Church and decide to be baptized.

Because I'm only ten years old, I need my dad's permission to be baptized. After my lesson with the missionaries, we decide to call my dad to ask for his permission. I'm really nervous and not quite sure what to say, so my mother does most of the talking for me. We place my dad on speakerphone, and everyone is eagerly waiting to hear his response, but he immediately says no—end of discussion. My dad is very protective of me and thinks my mother's decision to become Mormon was foolish, and he doesn't want me to follow in her footsteps. My dad thinks Mormons have weird beliefs, and he definitely doesn't agree with them. I'm not even sure where he got his information about Mormons, but apparently he knows (or thinks he knows) what Mormons believe. He thinks it's wrong for a religion to make you wear special underwear, tell you what to eat or drink, and take your money. But I know he just doesn't understand it. Since my dad and I are so alike, he doesn't want me to do anything to make myself different from him. I'm disappointed by his answer, but I decide not to worry much about it. My mother and the missionaries are disappointed too. She tries to talk to my dad about it, but she can't change his mind, and I'm fine with that. I still enjoy going to church every Sunday with my mother, even though I'm not Mormon like all the other kids. I don't need to be Mormon to go to their church, but I'm glad that my dad at least allows me to do that.

My Joseph Smith Experience

"A testimony does not burst upon us suddenly.
Rather it grows, as Alma said, from a seed of faith."

—*Boyd K. Packer*[1]

I continue going to church with my mother for the next couple of years, and when I turn twelve, I join the other Mormon girls at a summer camp—girls' camp. I'm nervous to be gone for so many days, especially as I've never even had one-night sleepovers before. I've never been camping, and I don't consider myself an outdoorsy kind of person. I'm also nervous about being stuck with people I don't know. I really like some of the older girls from my ward, but I won't be around them much because I'm not in their age group. Even though I've been going to the Mormon Church for a couple years now, I'm still not an actual Mormon, and I wasn't raised like these other girls.

Despite my worries, I pack up and join the other girls at the camp, which is held a few hours away in Seneca, New York. Shortly after arriving at camp, I start to bond with one of my camp leaders and some of the other girls from different wards, and I begin to think that maybe this won't be so bad. While we're at camp, we have the privilege to attend a special performance known as the Hill Cumorah Pageant. It's a colorful and energetic performance put on by members of the Church about the Book of Mormon and Resurrection of Jesus Christ. I haven't read the Book of Mormon, so I'm not familiar with the stories the performance depicts, but it's very powerful all the same.

While we're there in Palmyra, we walk through a forest known as the Sacred Grove. This is where Joseph Smith came to pray to ask God his questions, and God and Jesus Christ came and spoke with him. As I walk through these green woods, I can tell there's something special about being there. A happy, warm, peaceful feeling touches my heart. Afterward, we visit a log home that was rebuilt to resemble the prophet Joseph Smith's childhood home. I'm taught that this is the place where the angel Moroni came to visit Joseph. Standing in this bedroom, I am in awe that an angel once stood here. Again, I feel that same happy feeling in my heart. It's a familiar feeling to me. I've had experiences where I have felt a warm, loving, comforting, happy feeling when I've been scared or sad. In those moments, I know it is God comforting me. I can almost feel Him hugging me, letting me know everything will be okay. As I visit these special places, I get this same feeling.

Each morning at girls' camp, everyone reads scriptures and writes in their journals. This is the first time I've ever read the scriptures on my own, and after visiting those historic sites, I decide I want to read more about Joseph Smith. (Plus, it's also a lot easier for me to understand Joseph Smith—History than the rest of the scriptures.) As I read, I can't help but believe the story I'm reading. Joseph Smith was taught the Bible by his mother, and he had faith. He knew he believed in something, in Someone, but he wanted to know more. There was so much conversation about religion at the time in 1820, and he was confused about what to do. So he walked into that beautiful green forest, the Sacred Grove, and knelt down to pray and find out which church was true. God and Jesus Christ came and spoke to Joseph Smith, right there in that same spot in the forest that I walked through. They told him none of the churches on the earth were completely true and that he needed to restore Christ's Church to the earth. After Christ and His Apostles died, men changed the teachings and corrupted the gospel and organization of the Church. After some time, there was no more priesthood authority from Christ on the earth. The Bible was changed and corrupted, and many different churches were formed. There were no prophets or apostles on the earth anymore until Joseph Smith was asked to restore Christ's Church and was given that priesthood authority.

Because I've had spiritual experiences as a child myself, it doesn't surprise me to read about Joseph's experiences as a young person too. I believe it's possible for God to come and communicate with us. He loves us, so why wouldn't He talk to us? We talk to Him when we pray, so it would only make sense for Him to communicate back. As there have been prophets of God throughout history, of course it makes sense that we would be given a prophet to lead us today. And to me, it just makes sense that God and Jesus have bodies and are two separate people. After all, Jesus is God's son. Even before my mother joined the Mormon Church, she still taught me about prayers and put me in Catechism (basically Catholic Sunday school) so I could learn about the Bible. I'd believed in God and Jesus my whole life before going to the Mormon Church.

I have a great time with all these girls at girls' camp, and I learn a lot from reading the scriptures and from the lessons I participate in. Everything I'm learning feels right. At the end of the week, we all gather together one night for a big testimony meeting. As I sit with the other girls, I'm nervous, but I feel the need to share my feelings. I listen to all these other girls crying and sharing their experiences from the week and how their hearts have been touched. In the dark, I walk past the rows of girls up to the blazing fire to bear my testimony of the Spirit I felt in those sacred places and in the story known as the First Vision. I know for sure that Joseph Smith was a prophet called of God. I believe God came to him and told him how to restore the Church. I know he was given the ability from God to translate the Book of Mormon. Even though I'm not Mormon, I know the things I've learned are true.

TIME TO ACT

Over the next three years, I learn more about the Mormon Church and Joseph Smith and I attend every possible Church activity. I love watching videos about Joseph Smith, and that's the thing about the Church I believe in the strongest. I make some of my best friends at church, but unfortunately they don't go to my school because they all live by my mother, and I live in a different town with my dad. I attend Especially for Youth, youth conference, and Mutual on Wednesday nights, and I continue to go back to girls' camp every year. I act like I'm Mormon, but I don't feel a huge need to be baptized. My mother wasn't baptized until she was fifty-five, so what's the rush?

But this changes one Sunday in January, right after my fifteenth birthday. As I sit in sacrament meeting, a little girl is confirmed after her baptism the day before. During her confirmation, I feel overwhelmed with jealousy and a desire to have the same things she does. My hands get sweaty and my heart races. She is being promised so many blessings, and I want those same blessings too. I feel the Spirit so strongly as I sit there, listening to her confirmation. I know that I want to be baptized right away.

After sacrament meeting, my best friend's brother approaches me with a question. He's preparing for his mission, and he jokingly acts like a missionary already, asking if I want to be baptized. To his surprise, my answer is yes. I proudly tell everyone at church that Sunday that I'm getting baptized, and they're all so excited for me. I meet with the missionaries after church and begin my preparations.

On Wednesday, I drive with my dad to meet up with my mother so I can go to Mutual. Sitting in the back seat of the car, I gather my courage and ask my dad again if I can be baptized. His answer is the same as it was five years ago: *no*. I'm disappointed but not defeated, and I know he's going to take some convincing. I'm not a little kid anymore—I can't easily be coaxed in any direction. I know what I want, and I want to be baptized. I plead with all my might for my dad to allow me to be baptized. His argument is that I'm too young, that I just want to do this because of my mother, that I don't have enough foresight at this age to predict my future and know what I will want ten or twenty or thirty years from now. "You won't want to wear that underwear or follow all those rules," my dad argues. But I *do* know. He can't tell me how I feel—he doesn't know. He hasn't felt the Spirit teach him the truth. I tell him over and over again how badly I want this, how I do know what I'm getting myself into. I won't back down. I keep insisting. He argues with me, fights me on it, but I won't let him win. He can't change my mind. Finally, he tells me to do whatever I want but to make sure I know what I'm getting myself into, because he knows I won't want to be Mormon forever and eventually I'll change my mind. I'm so happy he finally said yes, even though he doesn't like it. I tell him he's wrong about my motives for joining the Church and that I'll never *not* want to be Mormon.

Finally, my baptism day arrives: January 26, 2008. My mother plans a huge party to celebrate my baptism. She offers to buy me a special outfit and arranges for so much food to be brought to this party, but I don't care about any of that. This isn't about a party or a chance for me to show off; it's a day for me to take a step closer to God and Jesus Christ and to wipe away the mistakes I've made. I just want to be baptized. Normally, I like receiving attention, but today isn't about that for me, and it actually makes me quite uncomfortable that all these people are here for my baptism. Even the missionaries who taught my mother come out for my baptism, but I feel so awkward! I wish no one was here.

I feel beautiful in this white baptismal dress, and Megan's brother is in all white as well. We take pictures together before the baptism, and I just can't stop smiling. I'm so excited and so happy to be doing this. But as I enter the font, I look around nervously at all the people gathered to watch. What if I do it wrong? All these people are watching me. Megan's brother smiles at me across the font. I think he's nervous too, but he and I have been practicing the baptism position where I plug my nose and hold onto his wrist. At least I know I can trust him and don't have to feel embarrassed around him. I'm here in this water because he asked me if I wanted to be baptized in the exact moment my heart felt that desire, and I'm so glad he did. I am the first person he'll ever baptize. The moment I am submerged in the warm water, all my nerves are calmed. I feel as if I am flying, like I'm light as a feather. I want to stay in this water forever. Coming up and out of the water I feel extraordinarily clean and joyous. It's a feeling that will only be replicated once: the day I receive my endowment in the temple.

NOTE

1. Boyd K. Packer, "The Book of Mormon: Another Testament of Jesus Christ—Plain and Precious Things," *Ensign*, May 2005.

Who Am I?

"I am out with lanterns, looking for myself."

—*Emily Dickinson*[1]

I t's so weird to me that I just took this huge step in my life to be baptized, and none of my friends at school really know about it or understand what it means. No one here even knows what Mormons are. I think it's really funny that the Church was started just a few hours away from here in New York, and yet the Mormon population is so small. There are a few Mormons at my school, but I don't know them—I'm not in their ward because I go to my mother's ward, and she lives in a different town, about thirty minutes away from my dad's town.

I have a boyfriend, R, who I've been dating on and off for about a year now. I can't explain to him how I feel about my baptism; he wouldn't understand. But he's helped me prepare for a lifestyle as a Mormon, even though he doesn't realize it. R encourages me to dress more modestly, to stop listening to inappropriate music, and to stop cursing. I am so grateful for his positive influence. I used to be popular and hang out with kids who did bad things like smoke, do drugs, dress provocatively, and get involved sexually with others, but when I started dating R, I stopped being friends with them, and he became my focus. Before then, I was so desperate for attention, which is why I tried to be friends with the popular kids and do some of the same things they did. But now that I have R, he gives me the confidence and validation I was looking for. He is so sweet to me, always writing me the most beautiful and poetic love notes. He doesn't like seeing me with those popular kids because he knows that isn't really me, and he understands and respects me and isn't like the other boys at school who do naughty things or lie to get what they want. He's a good boy and honestly would be considered a "loser" by the cool kids. But I don't care—I love being a loser with him. I feel like we're in our own little world, where all we care about is each other, playing our music (we're both huge band geeks), and doing well in school. We're good together—he makes me very happy, and I want to be a better person around him.

As we start dating, we're careful about our physical relationship. I've kissed several boys before, but I am R's first kiss, and he takes things very slowly. But about five months after my baptism, we go too far. Logically, I know I shouldn't have done it, and looking back I know it was a mistake, but at the time, it doesn't feel wrong, at least not in my mind. Since my baptism, I've started to compartmentalize my life. It feels like I really am living in two different worlds: one in my dad's town with R, where I feel like I'm not really Mormon, and one in my mother's town where I am Mormon. Regardless of where I am, I still believe in the Church, and I proudly tell people at school that I'm Mormon and I don't drink or swear. But at home with my dad, I don't have a reminder of the Church to make me feel guilty about my mistakes or anyone to be accountable to. I know my dad wouldn't be happy if he knew what I'd done with R, but not for religious reasons.

Yet I still enjoy going to church and Young Women lessons each Sunday and Mutual each Wednesday night. Even when I'm at church and church activities, I don't feel guilty about the decisions I've made that go against the standards of the Church. I hear lessons about chastity, and they don't bother me at all. I'm not sure why. If I know it was wrong, why doesn't it feel bad? I guess it's because I'm sure I'm going to marry R one day, so it doesn't really matter that this happened before marriage. He's the only person I'll ever do this with, so what's the big deal that it's before marriage? For the next two years, I continue to live in these compartmentalized, separate worlds.

Mormon Haleigh vs. Regular Haleigh

It's weird living two separate lives because they don't ever intersect. My Mormon friends are completely separate from my school friends, and I dress, listen to other music, and act different depending on which group I'm hanging out with. My school life is all about playing the flute, my relationship with R, getting good grades, and watching sports with my family. I'm more "preppy" in this life, but it's the most authentic version of myself—especially compared to how I act when I'm in my mother's town, when I sometimes change myself to fit in with my friends there. I love my life when I'm in my dad's town, but I do feel like I'm hiding this whole other part of me, the Mormon part of me. I don't talk about the Church with my parents or R very often, and even though I tell people at school I'm Mormon and have no problem defending my beliefs about drugs, alcohol, abortion, and pornography, I sometimes forget that being Mormon isn't just about what rules I follow. It's always part of my heart, but my actions and words don't always match those feelings.

When I'm in my mother's town living my Mormon life, it's like no one knows the other side of me even exists, and I don't like it. I'm very smart, musically talented, and have a great relationship with my dad and stepmom, but no one in my Mormon life ever sees that. My mother talks to all her friends at church about me but only about the ways I disappoint or hurt her feelings. They don't get to see the good parts of me; they only see her bias. I feel like, in the Mormon world, they don't really know me, just a small part of me that isn't entirely accurate. I thought I was special and I always wanted to stand out, but it seems like no one really sees me or thinks I'm special.

I'm embarrassed when R comes to my mother's town and enters my Mormon life, because I'm torn between which person to be. I also am so embarrassed by my mother's house because it's the complete opposite of my dad's house. My dad is a neat-freak and a little OCD, so everything in his house is perfectly clean and beautifully decorated. My mother's house is very cluttered, messy, and dark. I don't feel comfortable at her house, and I don't want anyone who knows me to see me in this atmosphere because it doesn't mesh with who I am. I don't want people to think my mother or her way of life is a reflection of who I am.

Plus, the Mormon world has its own lingo and culture, and it's just so different from the regular world. When R comes to church dances with me, I feel super uncomfortable because real life isn't the same as Mormon life. He doesn't ever see this other side of me, who I am when I'm with my Mormon friends, and I don't like it when I have to combine these two worlds. Mormon culture aside, my Mormon friends' personalities are completely different from my school friends' personalities. I feel like each side knows different parts of me, but no one knows the whole me.

NOTE

1. Emily Dickinson, letter to Dr. and Mrs. J. G. Holland, in *Letters of Emily Dickinson* (Boston: Roberts Brothers, 1894), 167.

Striving for Eternity

"There is no more important commitment
in time or in eternity than marriage."

—Henry B. Eyring[1]

A Future with R

By the time I turn seventeen, R and I have been together for an amazing three years, and we're more in love than ever. We're in almost all the same classes at school, and after school, we spend most of our time together. We go on walks, play outside, do our homework together, play music together, watch movies, and talk about anything and everything. I guess that's one of the perks of living in the same neighborhood as your best friend! We've discussed and planned our future together, and it feels like we're already married. I love when I get to make us dinner—it makes me feel like a wife taking care of my husband. I can't wait to actually marry R. It's time to start preparing for college applications, but we already know what we're going to do. We're going to music school here in New York where we will live together, and then when we graduate we will get married and both be band teachers.

Music is such a part of my soul, but I've always loved children and want to help them somehow. I think that teaching kids music will help keep them out of trouble. I see how kids are getting into drinking and drugs at younger and younger ages, and I want to help them stay away from bad influences and make good decisions. Most of my friends are in band with me, and they're all very smart and make good decisions. I hope if I can help kids become passionate about music, they can make good friends and good decisions too. I also want to learn how to play every instrument, and I get so giddy when I think about being married to R and always making music and having a musical family together. Being with R, playing music, and helping others are my greatest passions.

R and I are so similar, but our biggest difference is our religious beliefs. Whenever we talk about our religions, it always ends in an argument. I am so defensive and passionate about the Church, and I get so flustered and emotional when people fight with me about it. Even though I might not be following all the rules, I still believe the Church is true, and it hurts my heart when people tell me it isn't.

I've told R what the Mormon standards are and what rules I need to follow. He pretty much agrees with all of them, but he's never been interested in the Church. R is Methodist and likes his religion because he says it's really laid back compared to Mormonism. They don't have rules or tell you what to do—you just have to be a good person. That doesn't really make sense to me. What does being a good person mean? Just following the Ten Commandments? But I do think R is a good person. He isn't into drinking, swearing, drugs, or anything bad. And even though we disagree on religions, I'm grateful he respects me.

Turning toward the Temple

The Sunday after my seventeenth birthday, my bishop randomly approaches me and asks me to meet with him. He explains he wants to see how I'm doing, especially as I just had a birthday and it's the beginning of a new year. I agree and follow him to his office. When Bishop asks how I'm doing, I spill all the dirty beans. I'm not ashamed, and I feel like I don't have anything to hide. I tell him everything I've been doing with R (which I know I shouldn't be doing), and I openly explain to him how I don't feel guilty about it and have no desire to stop. Kindly, the bishop asks me if I've received my patriarchal blessing. I've heard about patriarchal blessings in my Young Women lessons, but I don't know much about what they are. He explains that patriarchal blessings are special blessings that are only given to you once. They contain personal counsel from the Lord, giving you direction and helping you to learn what God expects of you. Bishop also asks me if I've been baptized for the dead at the temple, and I haven't. Bishop tells me he wants to set a goal with me, a goal to repent and make good decisions so I'll be worthy to receive my patriarchal blessing and do baptisms at the next temple trip.

This is a big deal to me! The only time I've ever felt the slightest bit of guilt about my bad decisions has been during temple trips. I feel so jealous that all the other youth in my ward get to attend, and I just stay at home and pretend like I don't want to go, even though I really do want to go but I know I'm not worthy. I don't even know what happens in the temple, but I know I want to go. It sucks to want to do something and to know that the only thing stopping you is yourself and the decisions you've made. I have a tendency to pretend like I don't want something I can't have, even though deep down, I really do.

To do anything in the temple—even go inside the building—you need a "temple recommend" from the bishop, but you can only receive that little piece of paper after you've had an interview with him. The questions ask if you are keeping your covenants, if you follow the Word of Wisdom (the Mormon health code that tells you not to drink, smoke, do drugs, eat healthy, etc.), if you believe in the current president of the Church, if you believe in Jesus Christ, if you keep the law of chastity, pay a full tithe, and if you feel worthy to enter the temple. Mormons believe the temple is the house of God, so it is a very sacred place and "no unclean thing can dwell with God" (1 Nephi 10:21), which is why you need to be clean and worthy to enter. Of course, no one is perfect, but we need to be doing our best and feel worthy to enter the temple. Once I repent and feel worthy, I can receive that recommend.

After talking to the bishop, I'm so excited. I have the opportunity to go to the temple if I do what I'm supposed to. Even though I'm not worthy to enter the temple right now, the bishop teaches me that I still have worth. With the help of my bishop and Christ's Atonement, I can repent of my mistakes and become clean and worthy to go. I agree to this with my bishop, and I'm excited that I have a goal to work toward.

When I come home from that meeting with my bishop and tell R that we need to stop doing inappropriate things, he completely agrees. I'm shocked but even more in love with him because of this response. He tells me he knows we shouldn't have been doing those things, especially because I'm Mormon. And he's totally willing to stop doing naughty things with me. I feel relieved and so happy that I have such a great guy who doesn't pressure me to do things I shouldn't be doing. To my surprise, it's pretty easy to change my wrong behavior.

Next thing I know it's March, and I'm meeting with Bishop again for the interview to receive my patriarchal blessing. I don't know what to expect from this blessing, but I'm excited for it. Because R and I do everything together, I bring R along to my patriarch's house. But when it's time for my blessing, I am the only one in the room with the patriarch. He's in the same ward as I am, and I'm close with his family. Even though he does know me, as he lays his hands on my head and begins to speak, it is extremely evident that my patriarchal blessing is coming from God, not from the patriarch himself. There's no way he could be making this up on his own, and I can feel the Spirit very strongly. I am in awe at the words being spoken. I just sit there smiling with my eyes closed the whole time, soaking up every little thing he says. But one thing he says creates a pit in my stomach. He talks about the importance of my decision to be married in the temple to a righteous, priesthood-holding companion, and he describes the character of my husband. Wow. I'm speechless. Even though I've sat through many Young Women lessons on marrying in the temple, I never really thought much about it. I always imagined marrying R, and I guess in the back of my mind, I just hoped that things would work out and that we'd be married in the temple one day. But as I listen to the patriarch describe this man, my future husband, he does *not* sound like R, at least not right now. But that doesn't mean R can't become that person. That night I realize that my next goal is to teach R the gospel and have him get baptized so we can be married in the temple.

The ward temple trip is just a few weeks later, and I am so nervous. I have no idea what to expect at the temple. I know when you do baptisms for the dead you are providing the opportunity for a person on the other side to accept the gospel if they want to, as they've been taught about it in the Spirit World. Mormons believe baptism is essential to get to the highest kingdom of glory in heaven, so baptisms for the dead provide that essential step for people who didn't have the opportunity on earth. I believe this is true and important, but I'm still nervous about the whole thing because what goes on inside temples isn't really talked about (out of respect for how special and sacred the temple is). I enlist a friend from my ward to help me inside the temple, and she explains everything to me and helps calm my nerves. Without those fears, I'm really excited to go!

When we arrive at the Boston Temple, we get changed into all-white outfits, similar to the one I wore at my own baptism, and everything is so clean, calm, and beautiful. Everyone here is so helpful, happy, and kind. As I enter the water to be baptized so someone who is dead can have the opportunity, I flash back to my own baptism day. It feels like yesterday. I remember this feeling—wearing all white, standing in the warm water, anticipation building inside me for that moment when I go under, the moment when all the cares of the world wash away. It's just like I remember. I love this feeling. I feel like a different person now that I have my patriarchal blessing, have been to the temple, and am making good decisions. I feel so happy and lightweight, and I want to keep this feeling forever.

NOTE

1. Henry B. Eyring, "Eternal Families," *Ensign*, May 2016.

Goodbye, New York

*"You get a strange feeling when you leave a place . . . like
you'll not only miss the people you love but you'll miss
the person you are now at this time and this place,
because you'll never be this way ever again."*

—*Azar Nafasi*[1]

A few months after the temple trip, summer rolls around, which means another week of girls' camp. This year at camp, I'm a YCL (youth camp leader), and I feel a huge responsibility to be a good example to the girls I'm in charge of. I've always loved helping younger people, and now I have the chance to actually do it. But as I teach the girls about the importance of temple marriage, I feel like a hypocrite for dating someone who isn't LDS. One of the foundational principles in the Church is that our decision to get baptized, make good decisions, and keep our covenants all to prepare us to go to the temple and be married so that we can be with our families forever. A temple marriage is what makes us most like God, which is what we're on the earth to learn to do. I know I needed to get baptized, that was the first step, but now I realize that everything else about the gospel leads up to a temple marriage. Now I understand why Mormons talk about families and being together forever so much.

While teaching these girls only a few years younger than me, I feel a strong impression to break up with R. How can I teach them the importance of temple marriage when *I'm* not doing the things to lead me to the temple? I know what I need to do to get to the temple, and R won't help me with that. This impression weighs on me and eats away at me. When I receive a prompting from God, it comes to me as a thought or idea, like a gut feeling, and it just won't go away. It's this thing in the back of my mind that will keep telling me, "Turn around, don't do that, bring a jacket, you forgot something." I know God is telling me to breakup with R so I can eventually find that worthy priesthood holder spoken of in my patriarchal blessing and be married in the temple. I love R, but I love God more. I need to do what God wants, even if that means breaking up with R. God wants me to be married in the temple and have a family centered in Christ, and I want that too.

When I return home from girls' camp, I finally work up the courage to call R and tell him about this feeling that we should break up. I sob over the phone and tell him I don't want to break up with him, but I need to follow what God wants. R's reaction is unbearable; he doesn't understand why I'm doing this. I can't do this to him. I can't hurt him like this. I change my mind and decide not to break up with him. But still, I'm confused. I know I need to be married in the temple.

It seems like every Young Women lesson has been about temple marriage lately. When I hear people talking about their temple marriage or I see pictures from their wedding, my heart swells and I know I want that for myself. Some of my Church leaders have even had private conversations with me about the temple and R, telling me I need to be with someone who will take me to the temple, and I need to leave here and not settle for a life with someone who can't give me what I really want. But they don't even know him! I'm so defensive about R. I love him, and I don't want anyone to say anything bad about him or our relationship. I can't handle this pressure, and it's making me really mad that people are saying these things to me. They're not my parents—they have no right to tell me what to do, nor can they predict my future.

BYU? HECK NO.

As I'm finishing unpacking my things from girls' camp, I find a note in one of my bags from a girl in my ward who's a few years older than me and currently studying at Brigham Young University. In her note, she says she felt a strong impression to tell me to look into going to BYU. She says she sees my potential and knows it would be a great place for me. BYU, in Utah? There's no way. I don't want to go to a place surrounded by Mormons (even though I am one). I don't want to leave my family or R. I have my plan for the future, I can't change it. But I decide I'll at least look into it. My mother is, of course, excited about the idea of me going to a Mormon school with a good academic reputation. Surprisingly, my dad likes the idea, too. It's cheap, obviously not a party school, and he feels like it'd be a safe place for me. Since my dad and I are so close, I thought he wouldn't like the idea of me going far away, but he is very supportive. So that same summer, before I start my senior year, I get on a plane and find myself flying over the Wasatch Mountains to see Utah and visit BYU for the first time.

The first thing I *have* to do after the plane lands is see the Salt Lake Temple. After just a couple of hours in Utah, I'm already in love with it. It feels like a magnet, like something in me is pulling me here. I feel comfortable and happy, like I belong here.

The BYU campus is beautiful. The colorful flowers everywhere are stunning; the huge green mountains are breathtaking; it's so clean, and everyone seems so happy. I even run into someone on campus who served his mission in my ward back in New York. It seems like a sign. For whatever reason, this place just feels right. While I'm on campus, I meet with one of the flute professors to talk about studying music. But during our conversation, I realize I shouldn't study music. What is happening to me? My plan for everything is changing so fast! I always wanted to study music, and I never wanted to go to BYU. But during this short trip, I realize I need to do everything in my power to get to BYU, even if it means leaving R behind.

I haven't been successful in teaching R about the Church. He makes fun of the Book of Mormon when I try to read it to him, which really hurts my feelings. He claims he feels like all eyes are on him when he comes to church with me, like everyone is staring him down, judging him. He's probably right—all my leaders at church have told me to break up with him, so they're probably the ones giving him the stink eye. I hate this. Why isn't this working? He's only come to church a few times, but I've prayed so hard each time that he'll feel the Spirit. Why doesn't he feel what I feel?

I made a list of things I want in my life—the type of person I want to be and the things I want to have. It's attached to my mirror, and I read it every day. At the top of the list is "temple marriage," but it doesn't look like I will ever have that with R. It's starting to put a strain on our relationship. What will happen if I go to BYU and leave him here in New York? I doubt I'll even get into BYU anyway. There are several schools owned by the Mormon Church, so I apply to all of them in case I don't get into BYU–Provo. I apply to BYU–Idaho and even visit there, but it's definitely not my first choice. But even at BYU–I, I felt again like I shouldn't study music. It seems like my whole life plan is being rewritten. I want to go to a church school (hopefully BYU–Provo) no matter what, and deep down, I want to be with someone who's Mormon.

I put so much effort into my application for BYU and do everything I can to prepare. I've heard that BYU is very difficult to get into, that even kids with 4.0 GPAs, Eagle Scout Awards, Personal Progress Awards, Seminary diplomas, volunteer experience, etc., don't get in. I definitely don't feel like I've done enough to be attractive to BYU at this point. My grades are good, but I never put a lot of effort to get those grades. I never went above and beyond to stand out academically, only musically. I spend countless hours writing and rewriting my application essays. I feel like I need to go to seminary to try to help my application look better, but my dad won't wake up that early and take me, so I have to somehow find a car so that I can drive myself. Miraculously, someone from church hears about my cause and *gives* me her car so that I can go to seminary and hopefully get into BYU. I take a few AP classes to try to look appealing as well, and I put more effort into my grades than ever before.

A few months later, in the middle of my senior year, I'm sitting next to R on the couch at his house when I get a notification on my phone. It's an email from Brigham Young University admissions. I'M IN! AND WITH A SCHOLARSHIP! I can't believe it! I turn to R, ecstatic about the news, but as we look at each other, I think we both know our fate. "Congratulations," R says hesitantly. This moment is so happy but also so, so sad. I love R so much, but I know I'm leaving him to go to Utah.

I rush down the street to tell my family the good news. My parents are both thrilled that I got in. My mother always talks about me to other people, and now she brags about me being accepted to BYU. I didn't think I'd ever be accepted into BYU, especially not with a scholarship, but I guess being a convert from the East Coast did something good for me. Originally when I talked to my parents and R about going to college, we all planned on me staying here in New York, but now we know I'll be leaving to go out West.

WHAT TO DO WITH R?

I spend the rest of my senior year at war with myself. These past few months have been so hard for me. It seems like because I have all these good things going for me right now, R feels threatened, so he keeps criticizing me and tearing me down. Instead of being happy for me for the things I've accomplished, like passing my driver's test on the first try and getting a great score on the SAT, he's jealous and angry. Throughout our whole relationship, R has called me mean names; if I did something he didn't like he would call me a "dumb hoe" even though I wasn't doing anything inappropriate. I brushed the way he treated me to the side because I love him and I knew he didn't mean it. I think R held on to resentment from my popular days before we were together, so I tried to cut him some slack and understand why he might be saying these things. But as I look to the future and try to move forward with my life, R's resentment becomes much worse. I've always forgiven him for saying these things, but now it's really starting to affect me.

One second R says I'm so amazing, I'm so beautiful, and he doesn't deserve me. And the next he's telling me all these things I need to change about myself: I'm too immature; I'm too needy; I can't wear leggings/yoga pants/skirts/dresses/makeup because it'll attract the wrong attention from boys and he doesn't trust me. Which one is it? Am I not good enough, or am I too good? I can't win with him, and I feel like every decision I make is to try to please him and do what he wants. There's definitely a divide between us right now, but I understand why he's acting this way.

R and I fight constantly, and I find myself threatening to end our relationship all the time. I know I deserve to have the things

I want: someone who treats me better, to go to BYU and enjoy my time there without feeling guilty, to be married in the temple. But I can't break up with R, and I feel like I have to make the most of my time with him while I'm still here in New York. I can't break up with him before prom or graduation; I'd be miserable the whole rest of the year, whenever I saw him in the halls, in our classes, in the neighborhood. But I'm pretty miserable now. I've been crying practically every day, just thinking about leaving and being away from R. It's scary! I'm really excited to leave New York and go to BYU—it's become my dream—but I just don't want to leave everything I have here. I wish I could bring them all with me. Even though things haven't been good between me and R, the idea of being without him makes me so sad. I don't know what I'll do without him.

Time flies by. These few weeks of summer I have before my move to Utah are more difficult than I could have imagined. R and I are so busy this summer—he's away on family vacations, I'm spending time with my Mormon friends and packing for my move—that we hardly see each other. I've been hanging out with a lot of other boys this summer who treat me much better than R, but they don't compare to R. He is so incredibly smart, talented, and good looking, and he makes me feel something no other boy has ever made me feel. Now that the time is approaching for me to leave R, I realize I cannot picture myself with anyone more suited or a better fit for me. You would think that with all the Church activities I've been attending (girls' camp, Priest-Laurel conference, etc.) that I would be thinking more about temple marriages, but really I just want to marry R any way I can. He is so special, and we've spent such a long time together making so many memories that I can't throw away. He's been by my side since I was thirteen, he's seen me go through difficult times in my family, he's helped me to grow into the girl I am, and he's been there for every meaningful thing in my life. He means more to me than anyone else, and I can't imagine feeling more love for anyone else. But I don't know how we are supposed to live our lives together when we both think so differently about life and religion.

As I think realistically about what it would mean to marry R, I think of my dad and stepmom. My dad got remarried seven years ago to my stepmom, who is so amazing and acts like such a great mom to me that I even call her mom! Her son tragically died at twenty-one years old, shortly after she and my dad got married, and she's had to cling to her faith through the sadness of losing her child. My dad, on the other hand, seems to have lost any faith or belief he might have once had. He used to say he thought God brought him and my stepmom together, but now he says God doesn't exist. He doesn't like organized religion, and he chooses to believe in the science he's learned. I don't know how my stepmom can be married to someone who believes such huge, fundamentally different things. My dad believes when we die we are done, that's the end of our life and we just turn into dirt. But my stepmom doesn't believe that, and I would be devastated if my husband thought we wouldn't be together after we die.

I don't want to live my life like that. She is amazing for keeping her faith and not arguing with my dad about their different opinions and loving him regardless of their differences, but I could never keep my mouth shut like that—I'm way too honest about my thoughts and opinions and it would make me too sad to know the person I love doesn't think our family will be together forever. If R and I got married, I would have to do that; I'd have to be Mormon by myself and keep my beliefs to myself. I guess if it's meant to be, we'll find a way to make it work. But that makes me wonder where my loyalty to the Church went. Why am I willing to spend my life keeping the biggest part of myself quiet? I need the Church in my life, and I want the priesthood in my home. I don't want to do it on my own; I want a husband to go to church with me and raise our children in this gospel that I love. I've seen families in my ward who have fathers to give blessings when they're sick or to start a new year of school, I see dads baptizing their eight-year-old children, I see families taking up a whole pew at church—I want all of that. If that tears me and R apart, well, that sucks for him. I'm just so confused about everything and so full of emotion with all the things coming up in my life. R and the Church are the two most important things to me, but they just don't seem to fit together.

The summer eventually comes to an end, and with it comes the time for me to say goodbye to New York and to R. I don't know how to say those words. I've been dreading this moment for weeks. I feel sick to my stomach; I don't know how to handle this. I love Utah and BYU so much, I really am excited to leave New York behind and go, but I just don't know who I am without R. Without him I don't really feel like myself, as I've been with him for so much of my life and he's influenced so much of who I am. How am I supposed to survive without him? I can't stop crying. I feel like half of my heart just got ripped out. How did I just get onto this plane? I feel awful leaving him behind. I felt so strongly about going to BYU, but I didn't realize how hard it would be to say goodbye. As the plane takes off, my old life stays behind and I'm off to a new stage of my life. I truly hope R and I will be able to make it work and will end up together when we graduate. But my desire for a temple marriage never leaves the back of my mind.

Note

1. Azar Nafisi, *Reading Lolita in Tehran: A Memoir in Books* (New York: Random House, Inc., 2003), 336.

"On You Go to Vanquish the Foe"[1]

"Can I start again with my faith shaken? 'Cause I can't go back and undo this. I just have to stay and face my mistakes, but if I get stronger and wiser I'll get through this."[2]

ADJUSTING TO BYU

My freshman year at BYU comes with a whirlwind of emotions. After saying goodbye to my parents, I feel so alone. I can't believe I won't see them for four months. Leaving my family, my friends, my music, my hobbies, and R behind makes me feel like a completely different person. I don't know who I am without those things—they defined me. I'm so homesick.

Arriving at BYU, I'm overwhelmed by all the changes. First of all, it seems like everyone here is from Utah and was raised Mormon. I don't fit in with them, and they can't understand me. Second, I hate the dorms. At home, I had a large bedroom, a big closet, and a whole bathroom to myself. This is not the case at

Helaman Halls. I hate not having a bathroom with my own toilet or shower—community bathrooms gross me out. As it happens, I arrive at our dorm room before my roommate does, so I'm able to get myself set up and adjust to my new living space. I brought so many things from home to help make this space cozier (as the walls are basically cinder blocks painted white). The wall right next to my bed is covered in pictures of R and all the sweet notes he wrote to me, and it makes me feel a little bit better to have those things.

Having a roommate also takes some adjusting. It's so weird for me because I've never had to live with my siblings or share anything with anyone. My roommate seems so different from me. She's from California, her parents are from Mexico, and her family is Mormon. We're very distant at first, but I think that's just because we're both homesick. But we quickly open up and start having fun together. We both love to sing, so we spend a lot of time singing to each other; she even asks me to sing her to sleep sometimes. We become friends with another girl in our hall, and the three of us stick together for the year. None of us really enjoys having a big group of friends, so we spend a lot of our time watching movies and hanging out, just the three of us. I come to really love these girls; without them I don't think I could survive my freshman year. R starts his semester much later than I do, so he's still busy enjoying his summer with our friends back in New York. But even with my new friends, I feel so alone and like an outsider at BYU.

D or R?

My first week of classes is so horrible. My schedule is terrible because I accidentally registered for upper-level classes—I didn't know what I was doing! I didn't have experienced parents or older siblings to help me choose my classes. I meet with a counselor to help me get it straightened out, and now I have entry-level classes that are better suited to my interests. I always sit in the very front for all my classes because I want my teachers to know me. I'm very outspoken and I like to participate a lot in class. In my sociology class, I end up sitting next to a nice boy, D, who is the first person here to go out of their way to talk to me. As I walk back toward my dorm after class, he walks with me through campus until I need to go left to get to my dorm and he needs to turn right to get to his car. He asks if I'd like to get ice cream with him, but I'm hesitant and can't help but think of R. So I make up an excuse and say I'm on a diet and can't eat ice cream. I try to leave, but he's persistent and asks me to get a smoothie instead. Finally, I tell him I have a boyfriend, but he insists we can go out as friends.

Over our smoothies, I tell him all about R, my conversion story, and how badly I want to get married in the temple one day. D recently got home from his mission in Chile, and I can feel the Spirit so strongly with him. There is such a light shining from him, such a happy feeling as he talks about his mission and what he wants for his life. I didn't even know guys like this existed. D tell me about his love for children and his niece and nephew, how he can't wait to be a husband and father, and his love for the Book of Mormon and the gospel. He is so different from R. I feel so much happier when I'm spending time with D.

Over the next few weeks, he drives me all around Provo and Utah County, and we do many fun things together. It's so nice to get out of the dorms and actually do fun things like hiking, bowling, going to the temple, etc. At one point, D takes me to meet his parents, and I realize how badly I really want an LDS family. There really is such a happiness that comes from Mormon families, and even being in their homes I can feel the Spirit. I have to confront the truth: marrying R will not lead to a happy LDS family like D's. I decide I can't stay with R, no matter how much I love him. Plus, being at BYU provides a great opportunity to meet returned missionaries like D, someone who could take me to the temple.

This isn't an easy decision. I feel awful—R has been messaging me for the past two days, but I've been so confused about my feelings that I haven't responded. And I feel guilty that I've been spending so much time with D. I'm not attracted to D, and we don't have much in common, other than the fact that we both love the gospel and want to be married so badly. I have a breakdown one night with D, and I tell him how confused I am. I want to be married in the temple so badly, but I love R so much. D convinces me to breakup with R so that I can give him a chance. As I think this over, I'm reminded of what my other friends have been telling me: that I deserve to be treated better and have a temple marriage. So then and there I work up the courage to call R and break up with him. Predictably, R doesn't take the news well. After all we've been through together, he feels so betrayed and angry. He sobs and yells at me, and I'm crying too. I hate doing this, but I know it's the only way to get what I really want, and I could never have gained the courage to break up with him while I was in New York. It's now or never. I need to end this while I'm in Utah and I have someone else who could give me what I truly want. R can't give me the things I want. He is never going to accept the gospel or take me to the temple, but D could.

For a couple of weeks after the breakup, I try dating D, and I really think I could marry him. I never even told my dad I broke up with R, which is crazy because my dad and I are so close. But I've been so caught up in this world in Utah with D, and I don't want any distractions from New York. I finally call my dad and tell him I broke up with R and want to marry D. This is all so shocking to my dad, especially since he doesn't even know who D is, but I'm just so happy at the prospect of getting married in the temple. Even though he wasn't expecting this, my dad is glad that I'm happy and have someone taking care of me. Whenever I have doubts about D, I remind myself how happy I am. I try to talk myself into staying with D so that I can get married in the temple, but there's a huge part of me that's still in love with R. I'm not attracted to D like I was to R. He doesn't make me laugh or understand me like R did. But I push that aside and think about marrying D in the temple. One day, we Skype my dad so he and D can "meet," but on that call, all my dad can see is the lack of chemistry between us.

What have I done? I gave up someone I've spent so much of my life with, someone whom I love so dearly. This was a huge mistake. I'm honest with D and tell him that I still love R, so D and I decide to just be friends. I need to fix my mistake. I call R and tell him it was a mistake and I want him back. To be honest, I'm surprised he even answers the phone. He tells me he forgives me, but we can't be together again. I've broken his heart. He tells me that when he found out I was dating D, he was devastated. He agrees to be my friend but nothing more. I'm so depressed about my decision that I hate myself every day for it. R was my best friend, not just my boyfriend. I feel like I've lost everything.

When I go home for Christmas, I visit R, but just as a friend. It kills me inside to see him. I do everything in my power to convince him to give me another chance. I show him things I've written in my journal about how regretful I am, pictures of us, and memories of our amazing three years together to try to remind him of how special our relationship was. But he refuses to be anything but my friend. I know he still loves me, I can tell. I wish he'd just give in and let me have another chance. I can't believe I ruined the amazing relationship we had. I hate myself for putting us in this position.

A NEW YEAR, A NEW START

After Christmas break, I arrive back in Provo for the next semester, hoping it'll be better than the first. My nineteenth birthday is so different from my eighteenth. I'm not surrounded by my best friends, R, or my family. No one cares about me out here like they did in New York. I felt special when I was in New York; I felt like I stood out and had a purpose. I was so good at the flute, but now I never play, and even if I wanted to, practically everyone here can play a musical instrument and sing—and probably better than I can. In high school, I got good grades without even trying, but everyone here is so much smarter than me and gets better grades than I do. In New York, I felt special as a convert to the Church, but people here are way more spiritual than I am. Even though R criticized me, I still knew he loved me. But here I feel like no one loves me. I feel even lonelier than I've ever been, but I try to be positive: I'm on the other side of the country, in *Utah* at *BYU*! I need to take advantage of all the opportunities out here. I need to focus on myself—that's what college is for. I'm so used to having my whole world revolve around R that I don't even know how to be just me. It was always "Haleigh and R." How do I become just Haleigh? I have my moments when I'm homesick, sad, regretful, and confused. But there are also so many other times— in my classes, walking around the beautiful campus, hanging around my new friends, doing college things—when I truly do feel so happy.

There have been several occasions during my freshman year when I've felt God in my life, sending tender mercies to help me feel less lonely. I needed my thoughts to be straightened out, my testimony to grow, to feel my Heavenly Father's love, and to feel happiness. That has happened for me over and over again. Although the beginning of this new semester is difficult, I think back to Thanksgiving, which I spent with a friend's aunt and uncle here in Utah County. She and her uncle's family helped me so much. I had told my friend's uncle about my recent struggles, and he told me to close my eyes, then walked me over to a spot in his house. Finally he told me to stop and open my eyes. When I opened my eyes, my face was practically against the wall. "What do you see?" he asked. Nothing, really, just some jumbled colors. He moved me back a few inches. Looking right in front of me, I still couldn't really see much, I couldn't tell what I was looking at. He moves me back a couple feet, and tears instantly begin to swell in my eyes. It was a painting of my Savior. My friend's uncle gently explained to me that Christ is always here with me, feeling what I feel, knowing my heart's desires. I can't see it sometimes, I can't see the bigger picture and understand His plan, but that doesn't mean He isn't right here with me. Remembering that moment, I realize I have to have faith in the Lord and trust that He knows best and that things will happen in His time. I have to go on with my life and try to be happy; regardless of the heartache I may feel, I need to do my best to be happy and do what is right. I absolutely love the gospel of Jesus Christ. I am proud to be LDS, and I know that this is who I need to be and where I need to be.

I feel like I have been down for months, stuck in a dark, gloomy cloud that I couldn't get out of. But now I have finally woken up. It was a hard decision just to come out here to Utah, and the whole year has been hard while I've been trying to figure out who I am now. I was lost, not knowing who I was without the comfort of things and people from New York, but I'm so happy I came here. I will never deny the gospel. I will always stand up for it and defend it. I gave up so much for this Church, and I will continue to do what I need to do to live the gospel and become a more Christlike person. I will endure to the end, no matter what. I need to make it to the temple to be married there one day. I just have to have faith that my

Heavenly Father knows my heart, knows my desires, loves me, and will do what is best for me in the long run. Hopefully those things correspond with my heart's desires.

Notes

1. Clyde D. Sandgren, "The Cougar Song," byucougars.com, accessed 18 December 2017.
2. Adam Anders, Nikki Hassman, and Peer Åström, "Get It Right," *Glee: The Music, Volume 5*, March 15, 2011.

"Moving On and Getting Over"

"It's taken me so long just to say 'so long.'
Maybe it's all wrong, but I'm moving on."

—*John Mayer*[1]

R and I aren't friends anymore—it was too painful for both of us. He kept being mean to me, trying to make me jealous, and I couldn't take it. As I try to put R behind me, I'm ready and desperate to move on and meet my husband. I try to have faith in God's plan for me, but I still hope that since I broke up with R, I'll meet my husband soon.

I've finished the winter semester and decided to stay in Provo for the summer. I move out of the dorms and into an apartment complex where all the guys are returned missionaries, so I'm hopeful I could meet my husband here. This ward is really great and they have so many fun activities, but I haven't really clicked with anyone yet. My friends from my freshman dorm aren't here over the summer, and I haven't easily made new friends. I got a job at a restaurant, so that's helping to keep me busy. But I wonder why I haven't met anyone who wants to date me yet. With all these returned missionaries in my ward, I thought I'd for sure be asked out on dates. I've tried to get to know several boys, but it always turns out that they don't want a relationship—just someone to kiss.

I'm so sick of feeling miserable and unwanted. I can never get R out of the back of my mind. No one compares to him— how smart he is, how talented he is, the way we were able to connect and have fun no matter what we were doing. I'm sure there are a lot of awesome guys here, but none of them want me. Sometimes I wonder if anyone will ever be able to really love me and if I'll ever find my eternal companion. Will I have my happily ever after? I know I can, but when? I have earthly parents and Heavenly Parents who love me more than I could ever imagine. That love should be good enough for me for now. And yet I always want more. Being alone is hard, especially when I've been with someone and have been loved for so long. To suddenly not have that relationship, that person who loves and understands me and is always there for me, hurts and I'm not used to it. I feel like I'm divorced, and I just want to be married again. I feel sad, lonely, and hopeless so often. I remind myself that doing what's good and right will lead me to my happily ever after. I don't have to look for it. I don't have to search. If I continue to do what's right, it will find me. This is what I keep telling myself, all the while still hoping every day that I will meet my husband. Every day when I go to my classes, I wonder if my husband is sitting here in this room with me. Every day while walking across campus, I look around me at all the returned missionaries and I tell myself my husband must be here, and it must be worth it to find one to marry in the temple. I hope it is, anyway.

Before fall semester begins, I visit New York again, and it just brings back all these awful emotions. I thought I was over R, but now it's clear to me that I'm not. It's nice to see my family, but it doesn't feel like home to me anymore. Now it's only a place of bad memories. I attend church while in New York, and I end up chatting with a boy from my home ward, C, who's about to leave on his mission to Salt Lake City (of all places). He asks me if I'll write him while he's on his mission. I've always cared about him and his family, so I'm happy to write him. Returning back to Utah and writing C brings me hope for a temple marriage and happiness. I've realized how much happier I am in Utah and that I need to leave everything about New York behind. I'm not happy when I'm there, and even thinking about New York makes me feel miserable. Reading letters from C and hearing about his experiences on his mission brings such joy to my life. I can feel the Spirit so strongly in his letters, and I feel so much love for him. C and I have always had a fondness for each other, but I was with R in high school, so I never gave him a chance. Maybe I'm supposed to end up with C and this was the plan all along. He is my patriarch's grandson, and I've always been close to their family. Writing C is so motivating for me; it helps me to want to make good decisions and help others, which gives me confidence and a sense of purpose. Plus it's really nice not to worry about dating anymore.

I have new roommates waiting for me when I return from New York. One of them, Chloe, is newly converted to the Church after growing up in Minnesota with an inactive family. Finally, it's so nice to have a friend who can relate to me in this area! Not only that, but she's so sweet and cute. Besides my two friends from my freshman year, I haven't had the best of luck with roommates and making girlfriends. I just haven't felt that click with anyone, that instant friendship. So far, my roommates have either been so extremely different from me or they've never been around for us to even develop a relationship. But now I have C and fun roommates, so I'm a lot happier in Utah.

I'll Go Where You Want Me to Go

In the fall of my sophomore year, I watch general conference at my apartment with my roommates. During the Saturday afternoon session, they announce that the mission age for girls is being changed, down from twenty-one to nineteen—*and I'm nineteen*. This is a huge deal! I'm really shocked to witness this historic moment. I have been praying for direction in my life—to know what God would have me do. It's clear to me now with this announcement what I am supposed to do at this time in my life. Sometimes my plan isn't always the same as God's, but that doesn't matter to me. I instantly know I am supposed to serve a full-time mission for The Church of Jesus Christ of Latter-day Saints at this time in my life.

I tell my roommates I want to go and they're extremely supportive and excited for me. I know that my experiences and testimony are meant to bless the lives of others in some way. I know this experience will be extremely difficult and scary, but I also know that God would not ask any of us to do something that we could not accomplish. I'm reminded of Nephi's response to his father: "I will go and do the things which the Lord hath commanded, for I know that the Lord giveth no commandments unto the children of men, save he shall prepare a way for them that they may accomplish the thing which he commandeth them" (1 Nephi 3:7). I know this will give me strength and prepare me for the future. I know this experience will bless my family, current and future. I am willing to sacrifice my time, my schooling, and the material luxuries I enjoy for God and Christ, because they have sacrificed so much for me. Jesus Christ paid the ultimate sacrifice for me, and the least I can do is sacrifice eighteen months to share His gospel with others.

I'm grateful to have the support of my friends, because the phone call with my dad doesn't go so well. He threatens to stop paying for my schooling and my cell phone bill. He doesn't understand why I want to do this—it doesn't make sense to him. It seems foolish and even idiotic to stop going to school and go who-knows-where, somewhere that might not be very safe. But I know it is right. It is a sacrifice I am willing to make, because I love God and I love the Lord. I will have to make many adjustments in my life these next few months to prepare for this journey. But it is something I am willing to do. I'm scared and nervous, but I also feel so much peace and comfort knowing that for once, I can do exactly what God wants me to do. If God wants me or needs me somewhere, I will go there. I am so excited to serve others and bless their lives in any way that I can. I will honor and be grateful for the opportunity I have to be a servant of the Lord and share His gospel. God's timing is wise—He is all-knowing. I will follow His plan proudly and become a missionary for The Church of Jesus Christ of Latter-day Saints.

I have been given life, family, health, the gospel, and so many other blessings. I know that God has a plan for me. I wish I always knew what that plan included and when those things would happen, but I *don't* know. I have to live my life in faith, knowing that God will guide me and put me where He needs me. As the hymn says, I'll go where He wants me to go, say what He wants me to say, and be what He wants me to be.[2] If God shows me a piece of His plan and makes it obvious to me what I am supposed to do, I will honor and respect that plan and willingly follow it.

I meet with my bishop to get my mission papers started, but he remembers a time we've met before when I've told him of my past mistakes. These are things I had repented of, but unfortunately, he tells me I'd have to wait a year before I can fill out my papers so that I can take time to learn more and prepare for the temple. There's a large painting of Christ on the wall right behind the bishop, and when the bishop tells me I can't go right now, I instantly look over to that picture and feel as if it is Christ

Himself telling me I can't go. It's powerful but reassuring. I'm sad and confused, but I have faith that it's what's best for me. I just felt so strongly that I was supposed to go. I was convinced I was meant to serve a mission. Is this just a test of my obedience, to see if I would follow the prompting? The least I can do is try to live the best life I can and be an example and help others. That will be my mission for now.

Valuable Lessons

One of the electives my counselor signed me up for my first semester at BYU was a family class. I didn't even know these types of classes existed! I learned different theories about the family, and I was able to see what processes are healthiest or destructive to a family. I loved it so much that now I'm taking several classes from the School of Family Life, and I realize that it's become my new passion. My family growing up was not perfect—far from it. But until I started to take these classes, I didn't realize exactly what was wrong and what I'd like to do differently in my own family one day. We take the theories we learn in class and apply them to our families of origin. By doing this, I recognize where my own family went wrong and what I should have done in my relationship with R.

I've learned so many useful things from taking these classes, like communication skills, boundaries, love languages, attachment, etc. This is learning for life, not for a test or a job; I'll be able to use this information in my everyday life forever. Not only will this help my own family, but I'd like to be able to help other families too. I always knew I wanted my own family to be different from the one I grew up in, but I now know exactly the type of family I want and what I need to do to have it. I want to help other people achieve the family life they desire as well. I want to be the best wife and mother possible; I've always wanted that.

Even though my relationship with R didn't work out, I loved that I felt married to R and was able to take care of him and give him my love. I feel so full of love, and I just want to be able to give it all to someone and be loved in return. I'm learning all the tools and skills—I just need to find my dang husband!

After a couple of months of writing C, I stop because I realized that while I loved the Spirit I felt while talking to him and I did feel a sense of love for him, I wasn't *in love* with him. I realize I'm still in love with R, even after all this time. It's been over a year since we broke up, but I can't get him out of my heart. I'm still trying to move on and find someone else (who's not currently on a mission) but I have no luck. I get asked on some first dates but not a lot of second dates. I meet guys who I see a lot of potential with, but they don't see it with me apparently. And no one compares to R anyway. Despite my best efforts, I can't find anyone better than him, or anyone who wants me.

I ask myself over and over again what's wrong with me. Who wouldn't want a girl like me, someone who is trying so hard to learn how to be the best for her future family? Am I too chubby? Do I wear too much makeup? Is it because I'm from New York and wasn't raised in a Mormon home like everyone else? Is it because I don't fit that picture-perfect mold of a Mormon woman who's the ultimate soft-spoken, reserved Pinterest crafter? I see all the good qualities in myself: I'm silly, I'm musically talented, I'm smart, I'm great with kids, I love the gospel, I look high maintenance but I'm really easy to please. I like who I am, and I don't want to change to fit that mold. I'm not super confident in the way I look, but I do love who I am. It's just frustrating that apparently no one else sees it. I see other girls getting married who are so childish and don't know how to do anything on their own—their parents still do everything for them. But I've been taught by my dad how to do things around the house and how to take care of myself. Maybe I'm not as great as I think I am. Maybe

I don't really have all these great qualities. It's really hard being unwanted, when all I want more than anything is to be loved and have a family of my own. I just can't figure it out! Maybe it's just that the right person who will see me for who I truly am hasn't come along yet. In the meantime, I'll keep studying marriage and family life and try to become the person I want to be.

Notes

1. "Moving On and Getting Over," John Mayer, *The Search for Everything*, Columbia Records, 2017.
2. See "I'll Go Where You Want Me to Go," *Hymns*, no. 270.

The Breakdown

*"And if men come unto me I will show unto them their
weakness. I give unto men weakness that they may be humble;
and my grace is sufficient for all men that humble themselves
before me; for if they humble themselves before me,
and have faith in me, then will I make weak
things become strong unto them."*

—Ether 12:27

TRAGEDY

The first day of December, I'm on Facebook and I notice people
from high school keep posting things like, "So sad, RIP." What
are they talking about? What happened? I message one of my
old friends and ask what everyone's talking about, and he tells
me there was a car crash and at least two people are dead, one of
whom is a boy I've known since I was in fifth grade. I feel sick
to my stomach. This was a boy who was on the football team
with R and who used to live in my old neighborhood—we rode
the bus together every day. This puts life into perspective for me.
His name was Chris Stewart, and he and one of the passengers
were killed after his car was hit by a drunk driver and sent rolling

into a median. There were two couples in that car, and only one person from each couple died. Chris died, but his girlfriend lived. Her love was taken from her, and mine is just sitting on the other side of the country.

My heart is very heavy for those who didn't get another day of life and for those who did but have to live without their loved ones. Not being physically close to the ones you love, not being able to hold them, is so hard, but having the opportunity taken from you is much worse. I have the opportunity to see the ones I love, however infrequently, and I can easily call or text them and tell them I love them. But many people don't have their loved ones on the other line to answer, and my heart just breaks for them. I can't let another moment go by without counting my blessings and reaching out to R. I know he hates me at this point, but this is bigger than our issues. He's still there in our hometown where this tragedy happened, and I need to know how he's feeling. I send him a text, asking him how he's doing amidst all this tragedy, and he gives me a short but polite response. Obviously he doesn't want to talk to me, but I can't shake this new perspective and need to tell my loved ones how I feel about them. I can't go on without the person I love, unlike Chris Stewart's girlfriend, who has no choice but to move on with her life without him.

Just a few weeks after this horrible tragedy, I fly back to New York for Christmas. Being back in my hometown, the reality of this tragedy feels even closer to me now that I'm here where this horrible thing happened. My best friend Megan tells me I should just call R if it's upsetting me so much. To my surprise, he answers his phone. I'm in shock, I don't know what else to say other than "Hi."

"Who's this?" R asks.

Seriously? He doesn't even know it's me? I feel like an idiot when I respond, "Um, Haleigh." He pauses for a long time before responding. He obviously wasn't expecting it to be me.

The conversation proceeds awkwardly. I'm shaking with nerves and trying to end the phone call because I assume he doesn't even want to talk to me, but R actually keeps the conversation going. He asks me questions and tells me stories about things going on in his life. The conversation becomes more natural and relaxed, just like our conversations used to be—even though I'm still shocked that I'm finally speaking to him. This is amazing! It's so good to talk to him and hear the passion in his voice. He's loving studying music, and I'm really happy that he's living the life we imagined. After the phone call we continue texting for a few days, and he finally agrees to meet with me.

BUILDING BRIDGES WITH R

I'm so glad he agreed to see me, but at the same time, I'm completely freaking out. Things have been so weird between us, and I just don't know what to expect. By the time I'm driving over to R's apartment and pulling into the parking lot, I've really worked myself up. My nerves are making me feel sick. I'm terrified to see his perfect face. He said he would just come down to the car to talk to me, but when I arrive he invites up to his apartment. This is so weird—his life is so different now, but mine is too. I explain to him how much I've learned and changed over the past year, but how I still love him. I feel like I gave my heart to him and never got it back, and that's why I haven't been able to move on and meet anyone else. R explains to me that he feels similarly, except he feels like he gave me his heart and I smashed it. There's nothing left to give to anyone, not even me. I feel horrible. As if I didn't already hate myself for inflicting this terrible pain on myself, I've hurt him badly too. Now I know there's no hope for us, but it seems like maybe we can at least be friends.

A few days later, R agrees to hang out with me again, this time without any pressure of discussing anything serious. We're just friends playing card games and watching TV. Out of the blue while we're watching some TV show, R tells me he's had a hard time without me over the past year and keeps dreaming about me. He told me that whenever he had a struggle, he'd wish I was there to lean on. He said his natural instinct is to come to me in any difficult time, including the car accident. When he responded to my text after the car accident he acted so cold, but he admitted that he needed me during that tragedy. He said he only let me go and turned me away because he loved me and knew I needed it. I pushed and fought so hard so many times to work things out between us, and he rejected me every time, but now he's admitting he was afraid that he had made the biggest mistake of his life by rejecting me. He was afraid it meant we'd never be together again, but he thought if it meant I was happy, it would be worth it. But I definitely was NOT happy!

R says he somehow still sees my heart and loves me, after all the ways I've hurt him. He starts to cry, and I just sit there in absolute shock. I haven't said a word. I just listen to him pour out his heart to me. He leaves the room to grab a tissue, and instead of just sitting here on the couch like a statue, I follow him and hug him. It's like nothing I've ever felt before. This hug is full of so much love. He looks down at me and tells me I'm beautiful, that he missed me, and loves me so much. He says he doesn't deserve me. WHAT? I don't deserve him! I don't know how he still loves me after everything I did, the ways I hurt him. This is the most miraculous moment of my life. This love we have is special, and I will NEVER do anything to harm it. I will do everything I can to be deserving of him and earn back his trust.

I never expected R to return to me, but I'm so happy that there's hope for us again. Too soon, Christmas break is over and I return to Utah, hopeful that R and I can rebuild our trust and friendship. But unfortunately, the greatest, happiest miracle of my life ends just as quickly and unexpectedly as it began. Within a few weeks of returning back to Utah, R changes his mind about us. On my birthday, he tells me how much he missed my presence in his life over the past year, how comforting I am and how happy he is to have me back in his life. Then he tells me to be patient, to believe that he cares about me, and to trust the process and believe that we can do this, that we can make this work, in time. He said he just wants to be friends for now, but apparently he meant friends who never talk, because he's gone completely silent. For months, I'm going crazy, leaving him texts and voicemails without any response. He told me consistent communication would rebuild the trust that was broken, but he won't talk to me!

After two months, I finally have to give up. I send R a Facebook message explaining the pain and misery he has caused me over the past few months. I tell him that I constantly wonder what I did wrong, why he won't talk to me, and why he would do this after he said he loved me and asked me to be patient and work on building back the trust.

Almost immediately after I send the message, R calls me. "I care more about what you need, not what you want," he says over and over again. He tells me I'm going to be an amazing wife and mother, but not with him. He says he loves me and hopes he isn't making the biggest mistake of his life, but he knows I need to live my life without him. He apologizes for ignoring me, but he hoped I would think he's a jerk and wouldn't want him anymore. Well, I do think he's a jerk for doing that, but that doesn't change how much I love him. As the phone call ends I'm not sad—I'm furious. I can't believe he's doing this to me. He doesn't get to choose what's best for me. He can't tell me he knows I'll be happier without him. I'm appalled at his words and beside myself. It's finals week, but I feel lifeless. I can barely get out of bed to go take my exams. I don't know how I manage to pass this semester, because I've slipped into a depression. I decide I need a distraction, something to get me out of this funk.

Soon after the semester ends, I realize this ward and my roommates aren't a good fit for me anymore. There's been so much drama in this apartment, so many lies and fights and against-the-honor-code activities, so many bad memories. I can't live in this apartment with the reminders of how happy I was when R and I got back together. I need to do something different. I find a new apartment and I only have one roommate, but she's never around so I'm alone all the time. I try going to therapy to work through everything that happened with R, but with each session I realize more and more how fake he was being when he called me and ended things. He didn't mean anything he said. He just couldn't handle keeping us a secret (he didn't want to bring me up, as all his friends and family hated me after I broke up with him our freshman year). He couldn't handle being far away from me and living in fear that I'd find someone else at college. But I know he still loves me. It's like Edward in the movie New Moon from the Twilight Saga—he pushed Bella away to protect her, but he truly did love her and want to be with her. That's exactly what R did with me. I won't let him do that. I pack up my things and decide I need to go home and show R that he can't push me away any longer.

BROKEN

By the time Mother's Day rolls around, my stuff is packed and I'm ready to move home to New York in a few days. I'm laying out in the sun with my best friend Megan, soaking up the last of Utah, when my dad texts me and asks if I know anything about R's life right now. Well, it's been a month since I've talked to him, so I guess not. My dad calls me, and it feels like a phone call you get when you're being told someone has died. I can just feel the bad news in his voice. Apparently my parents went out for lunch to celebrate Mother's Day, and they ran into one of my old friends who's also really close with R at the restaurant. They mentioned to him that I'm moving home, of course because of R, but my old friend tells my parents that R has a girlfriend, and it's serious. WHAT? Just three weeks ago he was crying on the phone and ending things with me, and now he has someone else? Was he dating her the whole time? Was his story, his reason for breaking up with me, just a lie? I can't go home if this is true; there'd be no point. I text R and tell him I need to talk to him ASAP. I wait and wait, and finally, just two days before I'm supposed to drive across the country to move home for R, he finally calls me.

I don't even know who this person is on the phone. R is cold and mean. "Everything between us was a huge mistake. You're living in a fairytale—grow up. I've met someone else and I'm happy. I don't want you. I don't ever want to speak to you or see you again. You're crazy. Leave me alone." I cannot even begin to describe the pain I feel in my heart. How could he say such cruel things to me? I still want to go home. I don't want to be at BYU anymore; I'm not happy here. I have never fit in here, I've never felt like myself, and I've basically been depressed the whole time, even through the moments of happiness. I already quit my job and sold my contract for my room in the apartment. The plans are set.

I'm ready to drive home, but all of the sudden there are huge storms in the middle of the country. Tornadoes appear left and right through the Midwest, right where I need to drive to get home. That throws off my plans, but I'm still determined to leave. My dad calls me and tells me I'm crazy for trying to drive home with the tornadoes and after R said those things to me. "No wonder R doesn't want you," my dad says. "You're insane. Who would want you? I don't. You're not welcome here." Just another slap in the face. That's it: the plan is over. I have nowhere to go. I'm stuck in Utah.

Within three days, my mother is here to try to rescue me, but I just want to be alone. I didn't ask her to come here. I don't need anyone. If I can't go to New York, maybe I should still leave and go somewhere else. I decide I'll transfer to Dixie State and move to St. George. It's beautiful and reminds me so much of Arizona, where I spent many happy vacations as a little girl. So my mother and I drive down to check out the school, but we soon realize I can't transfer there: they don't offer a marriage and family program. If I really want to study this—and I do—I have to stay at BYU. So I have no choice but to deal with my misery and finish school as fast as I can.

I don't know how to let R go, nor do I want to let him go. I don't want to give up on him, on us. There is something in the back of my mind telling me not to give up on him. I have to try to adjust to life without him until he comes around, but I just feel like I can't give up on us, like there's a reason why I feel so strongly about us. I know life isn't like the movies, but I have hope for my happy ending with him. I've thought twice that I was over him and had found someone else, so it's okay if he's happy in the meantime with someone else. If he needs to adventure and discover life with other people in order to realize he belongs with me, then fine. I'll still be here. I don't care how pathetic it sounds or looks; it'll be worth it to me to have him in the end. But each day that I wait is torture.

One day while sitting here in my apartment all by my lonesome, three girls and their families barge in. Apparently these freshly-graduated-from-high-school girls are all moving in! I'm not excited about this. I am going through a lot right now, and the last thing I need is these immature Utah-Mormon girls bothering me. But they're sweet, and with time I come to really like them. But even with a new job and nice new roommates, I'm still so broken inside. I'm losing it. I don't want to be here. Everytime I take a bath I wonder what would happen if I drowned—would R regret his decision? Would anyone be sad I was gone? I get the horrible idea to just get in my car and drive, and I don't even care if I drive off a cliff or crash into a pole. But the moment I walk out the door, my roommates are right outside arriving home. I fall to the ground when I see them and immediately start crying. "What's wrong?" they ask as they pick me up and take me inside. They didn't know about R, but I explain the whole story to them. Surprisingly, they comfort me so well and suggest I ask for a priesthood blessing. It's good advice, and their support and the blessing help me turn around. Even though I felt so low, to the point of doing myself harm, now just a couple hours later, I feel so much happier. Maybe there's hope for the future after all.

Sunshine and Shadow

*"Everywhere in nature we are taught the lessons of patience
and waiting. We want things a long time before we get them,
and the fact that we want them a long time makes them
all the more precious when they come."*

—*Joseph F. Smith*[1]

It's my junior year now, and I feel like I'm finally in a good, happy place in my life. I live in a different apartment complex now and I have great roommates (the same sweet girls who I lived with over the summer). We openly talk about the gospel and our testimonies, we all have the same taste in music and take great joy in having little dance parties together, we love watching cheesy romantic movies and eating junk food, and I feel like I'm finally having the college experience I should have had all along.

I'm in a new ward that I love, and I'm more active and involved in the Church than I've ever been. This ward is so musical, and I get to participate in choir and play my flute almost every week. Music brings so much happiness to my soul, especially the hymn "I Believe in Christ." Participating and serving in callings really helps me to feel a sense of purpose as well, something I've been lacking for a while. This bishopric is so loving and supportive and feels like my family, which is exactly what I need, as my family is so far away. I'm so much happier even at school now too. I love my classes, and I feel so positive about getting married eventually. I see my roommates going on lots of dates and people all around me getting engaged and married, but I'm trying not to compare myself to them and let their happiness get me down. I have things to make me happy that don't have to do with boys (unless you count my obsession with One Direction), and I finally feel like myself again. I would have once said that I felt more myself and more complete with R, but that's not true anymore. I was constantly trying to be someone else for him, and I felt like my only purpose in life was to belong to him. That's part of the reason why I struggled so much without him at first: I had to figure out who I was and where I belong without him. But now I know, and I am not defined by him anymore. I am free of him. My heart is free to be alone but happy. I can be myself and work toward becoming a better version of myself.

I read my scriptures and general conference quotes every day to help give me strength to get through this time of waiting for the thing I want most, my own eternal family. In the fall of my junior year, I listen carefully to general conference, especially President Monson's talk on trials. His words speak directly to me, to my heart. I have felt heartbreaking sorrow, and I've been tested to my limit. But now I can understand others who face such heartbreak; I can feel empathy for those who've been devastated and felt so abandoned like I have. I know there is something to learn from the trials I faced, and I'm still learning. One quote in particular seems directed specifically to me:

> Our Heavenly Father, who gives us so much to delight in, also knows that we learn and grow and become stronger as we face and survive the trials through which we must pass. We know that there are times when we will experience heartbreaking sorrow, when we will grieve, and when we may be tested to our limits. However, such difficulties allow us to change for the better, to rebuild our

lives in the way our Heavenly Father teaches us, and to become something different from what we were—better than we were, more understanding than we were, more empathetic than we were, with stronger testimonies than we had before.

This should be our purpose—to persevere and endure, yes, but also to become more spiritually refined as we make our way through sunshine and sorrow. Were it not for challenges to overcome and problems to solve, we would remain much as we are, with little or no progress toward our goal of eternal life.[2]

I think about my time at Brigham Young University, about the sunshine and shadow I've experienced and the progress I've made. No other place on earth is quite like BYU. It's like its own little bubble-world. I never expected to put music on the back burner and study Marriage and Family Studies instead. I never thought I'd spend so much time depressed about R. I thought for sure I'd easily find my husband here. I never expected to meet my best friends here or have the most fun I've ever had, especially not with younger Utah-Mormon girls. And I *definitely* didn't expect to fall in love with Utah and all its beauty. As crazy as it sounds, Utah has become my home. It feels more like home to me than New York does. I know this place like the back of my hand, and even though I've had the hardest moments of my life here, it's also the most comforting place for me.

THE BEGINNING OF THE END

As my last semester of BYU approaches, I start to panic. All of a sudden, I have to figure out what I will do for work after I graduate. One of my main goals in going to school was to learn how to be a wife and mother, and there's no money in that! I'd love to somehow become a motivational speaker and talk to young women, or teach classes about marriage, but I have no idea how that would ever happen. What will I do if I graduate and I'm still single? I return to my earlier idea of moving south, not to

St. George but to Arizona. I've always wanted to live there. My family and I always went to Arizona on vacation growing up, so it's long held this place in my heart as a land of happiness and sunshine (the opposite of dreary New York). But even with this plan in my mind, I can feel darkness creeping back inside me.

I can't believe I'm back in this place, where each day is filled with unhappiness, where the negatives of my life seem to outweigh the positives. I seem to always be stressed, tired, and worried. I'm finding myself getting annoyed all the time, so easily, about any little thing. I feel like I'm constantly in a bad mood. When I think about graduating and applying for jobs, I feel so unqualified and inadequate. The fact that I haven't dated at all scares me. Graduating without being married scares me. I feel so insecure, wondering why no one can see the good in me, why no one wants me. I remember only the good, how R really saw me, knew me, and appreciated me, but I don't want to think about him anymore.

I feel so alone, unwanted, and unloved lately. There must be something wrong with me; why else would no one want me? I was on such a spiritual high for months, and now I'm on such a low. Is there something wrong with my looks? Do I look too sexy, even though I'm modest? Am I too fat? Do I wear too much makeup? What is wrong with my personality? Why don't boys like me? Do I have too much baggage? It's not like I tell everyone I meet about my dirty laundry. Do I seem intimidating because of my intelligence, talents, or opinions? Or am I not as talented, smart, or funny as I thought? I hate feeling this way, but I can't seem to shake it. There are so many talented, spiritual, thin, beautiful girls at BYU, and they don't come with a past like mine or a non-Mormon-New-Yorker family like mine. Even though I think highly of myself, how can a diamond stand out amongst diamonds?

It feels like God isn't helping me, like I'm alone. I don't feel His love or His help. Why haven't I met my husband yet? What happened to those promises from my patriarchal blessing? I was promised an amazing husband, but I haven't found him yet. After everything I've been through with R, after trying so hard to meet guys and do what's right, I'm still not getting what I want. I pray every day, I pay tithing, I serve in my callings, I'm keeping my covenants, I'm reading my scriptures, I'm attending the temple. I'm doing everything I should be, and yet I'm not getting what I was promised. Obviously God changed His mind or something, because clearly that isn't happening anymore. I'm getting desperate, and I decide to take matters into my own hands. On Tinder (a dating app), I start talking to non-LDS boys. I'm not having any luck with the Mormon boys, so I decide to expand my horizons a bit. Why I go down that road again, I do not know. It was the hardest decision in the world to end things with R because he wasn't Mormon, and now I'm just asking for the same thing to happen again. Little do I realize, this time will be much, much worse.

A Future with J

I meet this boy on Tinder, J, who I'm really falling for. He's in the Air Force, so he lives up by the base in Ogden, but he comes all the way down to Provo to take me on a date. It's such a good first date! We go out to dinner and then hang out at my apartment, talking and listening to music. I already knew our conversation would be great because we've had really good chemistry through texting and on the phone. He knows I'm Mormon and that I'm planning on moving to Arizona when I graduate in a few months, but who knows what could happen between now and then. I'm so excited about this relationship. He seems to really understand me, even though we don't have the same religious beliefs. We really don't have anything in common other than our sense of humor and taste in music, but we still have a really fun time talking. He doesn't criticize anything about me; he seems to accept me just the way I am. I feel good about myself when I'm with him. I haven't found anyone like this before—R always criticized me or told me I needed to change, and with the Mormon guys at school, I never felt good enough. But with J, he seems to really like me just the way I am.

Things move fast between me and J, and I feel like I need to stop for a minute and think about where this relationship is going. I don't want to make bad decisions and end up in the same place I was with R. I don't want to be caught between wanting to go to the temple and wanting to be with a boy who can't take me there. I don't want to mess up sexually and do something I'll regret. As I think about the situation, I know J and I can't be together—there's just no way for me to be with a non-Mormon if I want to be Mormon. That's the whole reason why I broke up with R in the first place, because we couldn't make it work with our different religions. In order to get the things I want, I have to be with someone who's Mormon.

One afternoon while I'm hanging out with J, these thoughts and feelings I've been having really start to weigh on me, so I know I need to tell him what's been on my mind. I don't see how this can work between us. It sucks, but I know I have to break up with him. "I'm sorry, but I want to get married in the temple. I don't want to hurt your feelings, but I just don't see this going anywhere." He simply says okay, he understands, and stands up to leave. As he gets up to walk out the door, I reach out my hand and grab him by the arm. It feels like it wasn't even me grabbing him, like my body did it on its own. *Maybe God is helping me and He's telling me not to let J walk out that door,* I think to myself. *Maybe it was God who moved my arm to grab J.*

I feel terrified at the thought of losing J. I explain myself, "I don't know what just happened, but I can't let you walk out that door. I feel like everything in me is telling me not to let you go. I think we need to figure this out." We sit down and talk this out. J sadly says, "I actually came down here with the intention of telling you something. If you want to break up, then I'll go, but you need to know how I feel about you." I know what he means, and I feel like I love him too. We decide we need to take a break from all the seriousness and relax, so we go out to dinner, and I can't help but beam at him as I look at him across the table. Holding J's hand, I just feel so happy. I've wanted to find someone for so long, someone who really cares about me and actually wants to be with me, someone who I can love and take care of, and now I finally have that someone. He tries to tell me he loves me, but I stop him. I want to say it first. With a smile, he pauses so I can finally say those words. I do love him.

The Temple or the Boy?

Once again, I'm at war with myself, just like I predicted. J knows how badly I want to get married in the temple. He tells me he's willing to learn about the Church, meet with the missionaries, and get baptized if it's what he needs to do for me to be happy. That would be great—it would mean I get everything I've ever wanted, but I don't want him to do that just for me. If he's going to be baptized, I want him to really believe in the Church. I hope that he will gain a testimony and we will get married in the temple eventually. I try to teach him a little bit about the Church, but he doesn't seem to be interested in it. He's never been a religious person. I want to be a good example, but instead I give in to temptation and end up going too far with J. Why can't I just say no and stand up for myself and my beliefs? At this point, it doesn't even matter to me anymore. I love J, and I want to be with him. In order to move forward, I have to give up either the Church or J. There's no way I can be Mormon and date someone who isn't without breaking the law of chastity. I guess I'm choosing J over the Church. In the moment it seems like an easy decision; I get to be with someone I love and not feel guilty about anything. I don't think twice about the temple.

It's J's birthday, but it's not a happy day for him. He's out of town, so I Skype him to wish him a happy birthday. He breaks down and tells me how sad he is because no one in his family has reached out to say happy birthday to him. I feel awful and wish I could be there to hold him and make him feel loved. One of the biggest reasons why I've always wanted to be married is so I can just love and take care of a husband. It's just in my nature to be nurturing and loving. "My own family doesn't love or care about me the way you do," J says through tears. "I've never felt so happy and so loved by someone before you. You make me the happiest I've ever been." I assure him of how special he is and how much I do love him. Breaking through the tears, a smile comes across his face. "Will you marry me?" Of course I'll marry him!

We make a plan to go to Las Vegas and get married in a few weeks. This is insane, but I want to marry him, so why not just do it? But a few days later, I chicken out. I come to realize that I went from wanting my dream wedding in the temple to being willing to settle for a quickie wedding in Vegas. I deserve better than that—I deserve a real wedding at least, with family and friends and a dress and pictures to look back on. I buy myself a temporary engagement ring until J gets me a legitimate one. I feel pathetic buying my own ring, but we are still planning on getting married, we just haven't exactly figured out when. He has a lot of big decisions to make about his future with his career, so getting married isn't a priority right now. That's fine with me, I can wait. I just want to be together.

My friends don't really like J. It's obvious that he's taking me away from the Church, which (of course) is a bad thing in their minds, but they don't realize that I've willingly given up being Mormon. They're also suspicious of his behavior and wonder why he doesn't make more of an effort to see me. One day when I'm getting ice cream with my friend Chloe, I tell her about my plans to marry J. Chloe says, "No offense, but no one wanted to date you at all and now after knowing this guy for a few weeks he wants to marry you?" I am completely insulted, but I don't need to prove our relationship to anyone. With that conversation, my friendship with Chloe disintegrates, and soon the rest of my friendships follow.

Red Flags

My last semester of school has officially started. I don't know what happened, but J seems off lately. We make plans to see each other, but then hours go by without him communicating with me and we end up not getting together at all. I try to be understanding and not needy, but I haven't seen him in a while and it's starting to worry me. There have been a few little red flags (like removing our relationship status from Facebook), but I excuse away his behavior in my mind, and if I do ask him what's going on, I trust whatever his excuse is because I want to give him the benefit of the doubt. I have no reason *not* to trust him. We're both busy and we do live far away from each other. It's not like he can come down here and stay the night at my apartment (BYU has strict rules about their housing), and maybe his roommate doesn't want me to stay the weekend up there with them. We'll figure it out. I just wish I knew why he wasn't communicating with me. It sucks that I've learned all these things about communication while studying marriage and family life, and yet I can't control someone else and make them communicate with me the way I want them to.

Before I met J, I had booked a flight to Arizona with the intent to find a place to live and look for a job there. Obviously I'm not going to do that anymore since I'm staying in Utah with J when I graduate, but I plan to go to Arizona anyway for a One Direction concert, which I had bought tickets for. It seems like a huge waste and I feel so bad that my mother has spent money to come on this trip to Arizona to help me, but I had no idea I would fall in love and end up wanting to stay in Utah! The night before I leave to go to Arizona, I tell J how worried I am about us. He ditched our plans to hang out before I leave for this trip, and I'm really upset that I haven't seen him in almost a week. When I explain my frustrations, J comforts me. "I'm sorry I screwed up seeing you before you left. I know I suck at communicating and I need to do better at making time for you. I promise I'll be better. But just because I don't tell you all the time doesn't mean I don't love you. We *will* get married. You mean everything to me. You have nothing to worry about." I'm feeling good now, excited to go to Arizona, and happy about where I am with J.

Within a few days of being in Arizona, J starts acting weird again. It looks really bad, and I'm so embarrassed. My mother is here in Arizona with me, and she hasn't even heard him talk to me once. Why isn't he talking to me? He won't even call me. This is starting to ruin my trip; I'm spending all my time freaking out about J and not enjoying my time in Arizona. My "fiancé" isn't even talking to me—what kind of guy does that? It's also a difficult trip because I'm not used to spending time with my mother. I appreciate her efforts to help me, and it sounded like a good plan in theory, but this trip is proving to be a bad idea. I really wish I had J to talk to about it. I need my person to vent to! At least I have one night of fun at the One Direction concert to take away my worries about J and the difficulty of this trip.

On Friday night, J's Facebook location says he's at some townhouse in Salt Lake City. What the heck is he doing there? Who is he with? I call and text several times, but there's no response. I imagine the worst. I text my dad in New York (though it's the middle of the night there) and tell him how worried I am. I don't know what to do. I can barely sleep tonight. *Finally*, on Saturday morning, J texts me very casually, saying he's been wondering why I haven't been responding to his messages. This has happened to us before, where I didn't get his texts, but last time this happened he just messaged me on Facebook. I didn't get any messages this time. He calls me after I tell him how worried I've been and reassures me again, telling me he loves me and is excited to see me tomorrow. We make a plan for him to come over around noon the next day, once I get back to my apartment in Provo.

I can barely contain my excitement to see J that Sunday afternoon, because it's been ten days since I've seen him. I wake up extra early for my flight, clean my apartment when I get back, get all dolled up for J, and send him a text letting him know I'm ready for him to come over and can't wait to see him. I wait and wait, but I never get a response. I call, I text, I Facebook message—all with no reply. Is he at work? Did something happen? Is he in the hospital? I'm scared. I try to message him on Facebook again, but this time his profile is gone. What the heck? Did he just block me? This is so embarrassing for me. What am I supposed to tell people (especially my dad)? What will everyone think? Everyone knew he was supposed to be coming over right now. But he just disappeared without any explanation.

I pace back and forth in my apartment, bawling in my bedroom and then crying in the living room where I'm sure my roommates are super annoyed with me. But I just can't comprehend what is happening right now. Why would he block me? What did I do? Just twenty-four hours ago he said he loved me and couldn't wait to see me. Why did he change his mind?

I go to a Church activity a few days later with my roommates to try to get my mind off J, and everyone wants to congratulate me and look at my "engagement" ring since they haven't seen me in a couple weeks. I can't tell anyone that he didn't even buy me this ring and he disappeared off the face of the planet! I don't even know what to think about this situation. I'm mortified. I feel the same way I did back in high school, living two separate lives. I'm happy at church and the activities, but I know there's no point in me going anymore since I chose J over the Church. I'm a fraud.

I wait a week until I decide I *need* answers. I tried to give J space. I tried to be patient. I tried to come up with reasons why he might have done this, but I can't keep guessing anymore. I need to know. Who goes a whole week without talking to their "fiancé"? I drive all the way up to his house near Ogden, making sure I arrive before he would be getting home from work. As I sit in my car parked directly across from his driveway, I see J's white Mustang pull in. I don't think he notices me. He gets out of his car and as he shuts his door, he looks directly at my car, where I'm still sitting in the driver's seat. He ignores me and just walks right into his house. I'm stunned. He has to know it's me, he knows what my car looks like, and he looked right at it, but he's choosing to ignore me? Finally, I work up the courage to go knock on his door. I can't be shy now. I deserve answers. I stand there ringing the doorbell and knocking on the door for probably thirty minutes. I feel like an idiot standing there outside on his doorstep. Still, no response. I decide to go back to my car to get my phone and try calling him. To my surprise, there's a text from him! "Honestly, Haleigh, just stop." So my number wasn't blocked—he's just been ignoring me all this time. Are you kidding me? I am about to reply when out of the corner of my eye I see the garage door go up. J's roommate's black SUV backs out, his roommate waves to me, and then they drive away. How rude! I think for a split second about running after the car, but I decide to sit here and wait for an hour to see if they come back. I never see them drive by. What should I do? I guess I'll drive back down to Provo and deal with what's happened. J doesn't want me anymore, for whatever reason. I've given up everything for him, and now he's given me up and I don't even know why.

Notes

1. Joseph F. Smith, *Gospel Doctrine*, 5th ed. (1939), 297–98.
2. Thomas S. Monson, "'I Will Not Fail Thee, Nor Forsake Thee,'" *Ensign*, November 2013.

Hello, Arizona

*"And suddenly, you know. It's time to start something
new and trust the magic of new beginnings."*

—*Meister Eckhart*[1]

GOODBYE, TEMPLE MARRIAGE

What am I supposed to do now? The man I'm supposed to marry just disappeared without any explanation. Do I move on and start dating people again? Do I hold onto hope that J will come back into my life and we'll work things out? I'm completely gutted. I have no idea what I did to make him act this way toward me. What did I do to deserve this? If he didn't want to be with me anymore then he could have just said that. Be a man, don't just run away. It took me three years to get over my breakup with R, how will I ever get over this one? Is this even a breakup? Will he ever show up again? I feel so lost and confused. I JUST gave up the opportunity to find a job or a place to live in Arizona. I could have done those things while I was there, like I'd originally planned! Should I go with that original plan and find somewhere to live in Arizona, even though I won't have the opportunity to go back and actually check it out? I guess for now that's what I'll plan on, all the while hoping J will contact me and I'll stay in Utah with him.

The bigger question lies within, and it's one that I'm terrified to even admit. I broke the law of chastity (again). My hope for getting married in the temple is lost. I gave that up when I said I would marry J. I was willing to settle for a non-LDS marriage, either with R or with J. I would have settled. While my core beliefs in God and Jesus Christ have never wavered, I gave up the thing I want most—a temple marriage. I wanted a family of my own that I could be with forever, which is especially important to me because I'm not sealed to anyone in my family. I wanted a husband who held the priesthood, who could give us blessings whenever we needed them. A husband to sit next to me in church and feel the same Spirit I do. To have conversations about this gospel that we both love with all our hearts. I wanted to teach my children about the plan of salvation and our purpose here on earth. I wanted them to know they are children of God with a special purpose. Why am I so quick to give all that up? If I want it so badly, why am I so willing to just throw it away? Why am I so willing to live a lifestyle that I already decided I didn't want? Now I'm confusing myself.

Do I still want a temple marriage? Of course I do, but there is no way I'll ever have that now. Even when I was at the top of my game—going to the temple, reading my scriptures, attending every Church activity, I still couldn't find a husband to take me to the temple. I don't even know what a temple marriage means to me anymore. I want to marry J, and that doesn't include the temple. But I don't have him anymore, so I guess I have nothing to hope for now. I'm emotionally and mentally drained from replaying things in my mind over and over again. I can't stop thinking about it. It's just like when R stopped talking to me after he and I got back together. I went insane thinking about it every moment of every day. I can't figure out what happened or what I really want in my life now. I had a plan, and now it's ruined. The only thing I can think about is that Arizona has always been my happy place, so that's where I will go to try to get happy.

GOODBYE, BYU

My last semester at BYU seems to drag on forever. Spending three months here while struggling with my testimony is not easy. Each day I feel like I'm faking my way through life as a student—saying prayers in class, reading scriptures in class, writing papers about a testimony I don't know if I still have, doing my calling, etc. In one of my religion classes, I had to write a paper on a controversial gospel topic, and I chose civil marriages. The Church pushes temple marriage so much, and now I've researched why, but I choose to argue in favor of civil marriage. It makes me mad that the Church makes civil marriages sound so awful. I don't have a choice now: no Mormon boys want me. I fell in love with a non-Mormon. I'll never have a temple marriage. I've given up on that dream. I've started picking up shifts at work on Sundays, and I've stopped going to church. I don't know how to tell anyone what happened. I can barely make it to (or pass) my classes. I have no self-esteem, so I search for attention from boys on Tinder.

While on Tinder, I come across J's profile (which stings to see him back on a dating app), so I swipe right to see what happens. To my surprise, it says we're a match. Why on earth would he disappear from my life and ignore me, just to swipe right to me on Tinder? But what's more, he actually messages me! His message only says, "Hi." I respond, and finally I'm able to get a lame excuse from him as to why he disappeared on me. J claims he felt too guilty taking me away from the things I wanted so badly— Arizona, the temple, etc. I tell him I don't want those things any more, I only want him. But he insists that I deserve better and should live the life I want. It sounds like R all over again, deciding for me what I deserve. I'm sick of boys doing that. Why can't they just let me make my own decisions about what I want and who I love? Just let me love you! I explain to J that I'm planning on moving to Arizona after all and give him the opportunity to see me before I leave. We keep talking off and on over the next few weeks, but he never comes to see me. I don't even know why I'm allowing him to talk to me, like what he did to me is okay. I guess the fact that he still wants to talk to me at all gives me some sense of worth.

I withdraw from my friends, and my roommates turn into people I just use to vent to, not engaging in actual meaningful conversations or caring about their lives. I only care about myself and the pain that I feel. I spend the majority of my time sleeping, watching Netflix (while eating tons of junk food), and working, while constantly rethinking everything that has happened in the past four months of my life. I feel like a zombie just going through the motions of life without putting any effort into the things I do. I'm still on Tinder meeting new boys all the time. I'm surprised to find myself actually liking some of these guys. I want to move on so badly, but as per usual, no one wants a commitment from me. They all say I'm so pretty and so great, but they don't want to be in a relationship with me, they just want to make out (and whatever else). Part of me thinks this is just the modern world—people just don't seem to commit to anything anymore—but part of me also wonders if it's my fault that no one wants to be in a relationship with me. No one seems to like who I am, but they like the way I look. So in order to feel some sort of worth or value, I give in to the boys when they ask for inappropriate pictures. Being told I'm hot, sexy, or beautiful means there's at least one good thing about me. I hope their physical attraction to me will lead to an emotional attraction as well, but it never does.

Since there's nothing for me here anymore, I look online and find a house that's in Gilbert, Arizona that seems perfect for me—it's right next to the mall and restaurants and grocery stores, the price is right, and the availability fits mine perfectly. It seems like I really am meant to move there, I even meet people at my work who happen to be driving down to Gilbert the same day as I am, and they're going to help me with the move. This move is the one thing that makes me excited about life. For some reason, I really want to live in Gilbert near the new temple. Even though I don't really have a testimony anymore, I still want to be around Mormons (just not as many as in Provo). Just because I don't believe in the religion anymore doesn't mean the people are bad to be around. Finally, school is over. I don't even care about graduation—the day after my last final exam, I drive down to my new home in Arizona.

GOODBYE, CHURCH

I look at Arizona as a new beginning for me—a place where I can forget about J and forget about the Church. 2014 was supposed to be my year, but it didn't turn out that way. The year started off great—turning twenty-one, regaining my temple recommend after years of not going to the temple, having the best time with my girlfriends and in school—but then it just went bad. My dating life sucked, but then again it never really was good in the first place. I started questioning God's presence in my life due to the unfulfilled promises and seemingly constant disappointments. And then I met J, and my life was so happy, until he ruined it. Since everything happened with J, I really struggle to figure out what I want with the Church, with dating, my future, etc. I hope that Arizona will be a fresh start and bring some clarity into my life. But since moving here, I'm more confused than ever. I went to church my first Sunday here, but I don't know if that's what I really want. Instead of praying harder than ever, reading the scriptures, talking to my bishop, and searching for answers, I decide to forget about it all. It's just easier that way. My heart is too broken, and I'm too exhausted to put effort into repenting and trying to find a Mormon husband. There's no point anymore.

None of the doctrine of the Church makes sense to me anymore. I can't figure out what I believe. Why does my patriarchal blessing promise me a temple marriage to an amazing husband? There's no way a man like that even exists. I mean, if I couldn't find him at BYU, he probably doesn't exist. It wasn't R or J, that's for sure. If he does exist, there's no chance I'm ever going to find him now. I just left BYU, the land of young single Mormon men. In my mind, my chances of finding an LDS guy to marry outside of Utah are slim-to-none. But do I even want an LDS guy anymore? If I was willing to give up the Church and the temple so easily, then obviously it's not as important to me as I thought it was.

Hypothetically speaking, say things with J did work out and we got married and had kids. Does that mean I wouldn't be able to be with my husband or kids forever because we didn't get married in the temple? Mormons believe that only the correct authority of Jesus Christ can bind you together in heaven, and when you're married outside of the temple (not by that proper authority) then you're only bound on earth. Joseph Smith taught, "In the celestial glory there are three heavens or degrees; and in order to obtain the highest, a man must enter into this order of the priesthood [meaning the new and everlasting covenant of marriage]; and if he does not, he cannot obtain it. He may enter into the other, but that is the end of his kingdom; he cannot have an increase" (D&C 131:1–4).

Mormons also believe in separate degrees of glory, or heaven. "There are three kingdoms of glory: the celestial kingdom, the terrestrial kingdom, and the telestial kingdom. The glory you inherit will depend on the depth of your conversion, expressed by your obedience to the Lord's commandments. It will depend on the manner in which you have 'received the testimony of Jesus' (D&C 76:51; see also 76:74, 79, 101)."[2] So because I'm baptized and have a testimony of Jesus Christ, I can probably go to the celestial kingdom, but if my family isn't baptized and don't have a testimony, then they will be in a different level of heaven? That doesn't make sense to me. God loves us, and we are all His children. He wants us to all be together, so why would He separate me from my family? And then there's also my dad and all my siblings and nieces and nephews and so on—what about them? We wouldn't all be together because we're not all Mormon and sealed in the temple?

I've done baptisms for the dead in the temple before and had wonderful experiences, but I also know that just because the work is done for them doesn't mean that those individuals will accept the gospel or those ordinances. Joseph Smith also taught that "all who have died without a knowledge of this gospel, who would have received it if they had been permitted to tarry, shall be heirs of the celestial kingdom of God; also all that shall die henceforth without a knowledge of it, who would have received it with all their hearts, shall be heirs of that kingdom; for I, the Lord, will judge all men according to their works, according to the desire of their hearts" (D&C 137:7–9). So what if the temple work is done for all of my non-LDS family but they choose to reject it? I know they'll have the opportunity to learn and accept it, but what if they don't? What if my dad is sitting face-to-face with Christ and he still says no (a very real possibility in my mind, given the things my dad has said)? I would be heartbroken if I wasn't able to be with my dad or the rest of my family forever. It doesn't make sense to me that the God I know and love would do that.

The idea of multiple different heavens doesn't sit right with me, neither does the idea that unless my family all decides to be Mormon, we won't be together. Back when I was at BYU, I talked to one guy about my confusion with the doctrine, and he told me I wouldn't care about not being with my family forever. It would be the same as me living on the other side of the country and being able to visit them. That infuriates me even more. It shouldn't be that way! I shouldn't have to go to a different level of heaven to visit my family! I want a forever family more than anything, but I don't see it happening for me. Maybe you don't really need the temple to be with your family forever, maybe I can have that without the Mormon church. So forget it, I don't want it anymore. I turn my back on the Church and leave my Mormon life behind.

I am a new girl living in Arizona, a non-Mormon girl, in my mind. When Christmas rolls around, I return to New York, and I honestly feel free, free to say and do what I want without the rules of the Church restricting me. I can go out on Sunday, watch rated-R movies, cuss, and drink coffee and alcohol with my family—all without feeling guilty or having to explain that I can't do those things. I've never argued with my family about the Church, but in the past, they've occasionally made comments that have hurt my feelings. My dad always made fun of Joseph Smith—the one aspect of the gospel that I believed in the strongest—my siblings made comments about "magic underwear," and it was all so hurtful to hear. But now I don't have to worry about that! I finally fit in with them again. I felt like an outsider and not understood by my family for so long, but not anymore! They, too, seem happy to have me back to "normal." In Arizona I can be whoever I want. I figure, I can still pray and be a spiritual person without attending a church or being part of an organized religion, like my dad says. I'm not turning atheist; I still believe, just not in the Mormon Church.

SEARCHING FOR HAPPINESS

One day while I'm on my computer on Facebook, I realize there is an "other" section to the messages inbox. I've never noticed that on the iPhone app before. I click on it and find dozens of messages I've never seen before. I guess Facebook filters messages if they are from people you don't have any mutual friends with. One of the messages is from back in August, when J and I were still together. It's from a girl, letting me know she'd been hooking up with J and had found my Instagram. Only then did she realize he had another girlfriend. She called him out on it and asked him if he had a girlfriend, but he never responded and actually blocked her. She said she didn't want to step on any toes, but she felt I deserved to know the truth. Well, now I have my answer as to why J was acting so weird. He was cheating on me and lying to me. It all made sense now, why he kept ditching our plans and why he wouldn't respond to me. Why he removed our relationship status from Facebook, never posted pictures of us, changed the photo of me from his phone background—he was hiding our relationship. I text J and tell him I know everything he did and I think he is a terrible person. He responds, "How do you figure?" I don't bother replying. I am shocked and hurt, so I distract myself with the company of another man from a dating website to make me feel better about myself. J didn't want me, but this guy does, at least for tonight.

I keep trying to date to make myself feel some sort of worth. Someone *must* want me, right? I know I have lots of great qualities, but apparently no one else can see them. I thought J did. He said all these amazing things to me; he even asked me to marry him! But I guess I wasn't good enough; he wanted other people, not me. What is wrong with me? My whole life I've dreamed about being a wife and mother. I just want my own family. I want a husband to love and take care of and kids to raise. I know families bring the greatest happiness—that's one thing about the Church that I do agree with. Why can't I find anyone who wants to be with me? Why do I have such bad luck with dating? Why does no one want a committed relationship with me? I've been in love twice, thinking for sure I'd marry each person, only to be completely heartbroken both times.

I use multiple dating websites to have at least *some* human contact. I don't know anyone in Arizona, so meeting boys is the only way for me to interact with people. It's terribly lonely. I spend my twenty-second birthday completely alone, and it is the worst birthday I've ever had. I go shopping by myself and spend money I don't have, and then sit in bed, eating Panda Express and Ben & Jerry's while watching Netflix. The Relief Society president from my new ward here is nice and asked me to go to the movies with her earlier in the day, but I just don't want to deal with someone trying to bring me back to the Church. It won't work.

The day after Valentine's Day, I get a tattoo with the phrase "love fiercely" to remind myself of who I am. Being in this place where I don't really know who I am or what I want has been really weird. I'm not a student anymore, I'm not Mormon anymore, I don't have a job, I don't have any money, I don't have friends or anyone here who knows me—heck, I don't even know myself. I thought I knew myself and the qualities I possessed, but now I'm not sure of anything. But one of the only thing about myself that I do know right now is that when I love something, I love fiercely. I'm an all or nothing sort of gal. I'm extremely passionate on both ends of the spectrum. Right now I'm not loving anything fiercely, especially not myself. I used to think so highly of myself, and I was proud of the things I've accomplished, but now I have nothing. I don't have anything to be proud of. I've ruined my friendships, and I barely graduated from BYU because I almost failed a couple classes. I literally have nothing to be happy about, other than the fact that I'm finally living in my dream place of beautiful Arizona. I feel pretty much numb to any emotion. I can't really say that I'm sad because I honestly don't feel anything. I want to feel something, just not the pain that's tucked away.

In my search to feel *something*, I join a bunch of different dating websites and apps. But the non-Mormon guys still don't want me. I'd previously thought my lack of dating in college was just because the BYU guys were stuck up and didn't think I was good enough for them. I thought for sure I'd have luck with non-Mormon boys, and hey, it worked with J. But now I don't get anywhere, even with the non-Mormon boys. When things don't work out with one guy, I move on to the next one. I don't want to date multiple people; each guy I meet I want an actual relationship with, but they never want one with me. I get excited about each new guy, only to end up being used, and I just let myself be used. This isn't the life I ever envisioned for myself, but I don't know what else to do anymore. It hurts every time I'm abandoned by another guy I let myself get excited about. I don't know why I keep trying, why I even bother. Obviously I'm unloveable. I must not be attractive, fun, sweet, silly, or smart like I thought I was. I'm just so lonely and lost. I have no one and nothing.

I tell everyone I meet I'm not Mormon; even when people ask me about graduating from BYU, I tell them I left the Church and am not Mormon anymore. I'm talking to one guy from a dating website and explain to him how I decided to not be Mormon anymore, and he starts arguing with me about it! He's not LDS, but he previously dated an LDS girl who had said all the same things I'm saying: "No really, I don't believe it anymore. I'm really not Mormon anymore, and I won't ever be again. I like my life much better now, I'm happier now. I'm never going to be Mormon again." He tells me that the LDS girl he dated said all the same things. He broke up with her because he just knew deep down she really did want to be Mormon, regardless of all her insisting that he was wrong. Shortly after they broke up, she met an LDS man and was engaged to be married in the temple. Lucky her. The guy on the dating website tells me he knows I will follow her same footsteps. Like her, I insist he is wrong and surely I would never be Mormon again. But that girl and I have more in common than I could ever imagine.

NOTES

1. Attributed to Meister Eckhart, as quoted in Jennifer Boon, *Survive and Thrive: Dating and Being Single* (Leicester, UK: Troubador Publishing, 2017), 2.
2. "Kingdoms of Glory," *True to the Faith* (2004), 92.

Knock, Knock

"Sandwiched between their 'once upon a time'
and 'happily ever after,' they all had to
experience great adversity."

—*Dieter F. Uchtdorf*[1]

TURNING POINT

After a couple months of my reckless behavior with boys, I start to feel lonelier than ever. Fooling around with these guys doesn't make me happy—it's just a distraction and a way to make me feel good about myself for a moment. I have job interviews daily but nothing feels right. I graduated from Brigham Young University, and I can't even find a job to pay me more than ten dollars an hour. Wow, I really must be stupid or something, because I thought I'd be able to get a job easily. I knew I didn't have a clear career path with my major, but I at least thought I'd be able to find a good job to pay me what I'm worth (or what I thought I was worth). I'm running out of money, and I'm getting desperate for something to do with my life. All my friends are still in Utah and active in the Church, so our friendships have become strained since I started dating J, especially since I made it clear to them that I'm not Mormon anymore and don't want to discuss the Church.

It's so depressing to sit in this house by myself all day. Of course I love the warm sunshine and being able to sit by the pool in the winter (it's seriously paradise), but there's no substance to my life. I feel like such a loser. I just graduated from BYU, and I can't find *anything* to do with my life? I feel like the only choice I have to find meaning—or at least friends—in my life is to go back to church. One Sunday, I decide to go to just sacrament meeting, and when I walk in I immediately notice an attractive boy, who happens to give the closing prayer. I leave church feeling excited to go back and hopefully see this boy again. I do some creeping to find out his name, S, and add him on Facebook.

The next week, the missionaries from my ward randomly knock on my door. I'm shocked to see them. How do they know about me? I've only been to church twice in three months. I quickly tell them I'm already Mormon and they can't baptize me, so they should just get back on their way and find someone else to talk to who can actually be baptized. The missionaries say they are glad I'm already Mormon, and they want to share a message with me. I tell them there is nothing they can do for me, so don't bother trying. They explain that their purpose is to bring people closer to Christ, and we all have room to improve in that area. They're so annoying—just go away! Hoping it'll make them leave me alone, I open up and tell them all my doubts and issues with the Church. They challenge me to read the Book of Mormon for answers. Even though I've been a member of the Church for seven years at this point, I've never actually read the Book of Mormon cover to cover. I've attempted many times, but I always get stuck in the middle. I explain this to the missionaries, and they challenge me to read it from end to beginning instead. The idea intrigues me, so I decide to take them up on their offer.

Spirits Lifting

I am a quote person; I receive so much inspiration and motivation from reading any kind of quote. When I start reading the Book of Mormon from the end, I come across all these scriptures I've never read or heard before. They really impact me, and I need to keep reading more. I start reading quotes I find on Pinterest from general conferences, and each one hits me in the heart. I feel so uplifted by these quotes, like they are meant for me. All of the sudden I find myself driving to the Gilbert Temple on a daily basis, just to sit outside and stare at the beauty, and I feel an ache in my heart to be in that building. It makes me so sad that I can't go inside, but I also feel peace just sitting outside the temple. But wait—why am I sad that I can't go in the temple? I don't even believe in the temple! The following Sunday, I go to church again, and the boy I noticed before sends me a text that same Sunday night. What are the chances? I am giddy and excited again.

One of my best friends, Chloe, recently got engaged, so I decided to reach out to her. Our friendship was strained for months, but I really need a good friend in my life and Chloe is one of the sweetest people I've ever met, so talking to her helps me through this weird lonely phase. I explain to her how hard it is not having a job or anything to do out here. She listens as I tell her what a hard time I'm having, and she gives me some good advice. Per her recommendation, I decide to enroll in beauty school—something I've never thought about doing before, especially since I just spent four years of my life in college. I've always been good at hair and makeup, and I love the idea of helping other women feel pretty. I totally believe when you think you look good, you feel good. Beauty school brings new friends and gives me something to focus on for five hours a day. My nights aren't lonely anymore, and I can feel my spirits lifting.

I've made some friends at church who are helping me while I meet with the missionaries and study the Book of Mormon. They're not pushy or judgy at all like I thought they'd be. I can even tell them about all my scandalous experiences with boys (though it's not like I'm proud of what I did) and they don't hate me for it. I hate so much about Mormon culture, and they completely understand. I hate the fakeness, the judging, and the need to hide imperfections and trials. Life is hard and people make mistakes—that's what the Atonement is all about. But my new friends get it, and they welcome me with open arms. I'm really surprised at how much I enjoy hanging out with these Mormon friends; I expect them to think I'm a horrible person for the things I've been doing, but they don't. They invite me to Church activities and make an effort to hang out with me, even if it means just sitting at my pool with me. Suddenly, my life is starting to have meaning and joy again! But unfortunately, it's just the calm before the storm.

NOTE

1. Dieter F. Uchtdorf, "Your Happily Ever After," *Ensign*, May 2010.

Heyyy, Bishop . . .

*"Every trial and experience you have passed
through is necessary for your salvation."*

—*Brigham Young*[1]

COMMITMENT AND TESTIMONY

Even though I'm starting to attend church again, I haven't
fully committed to being Mormon because I still don't have
the answers to all my questions. I really like this ward and the
friends I'm making, but that doesn't necessarily mean I want to
be Mormon again. The whole gospel is connected, so if I don't
have a testimony about temples and their necessity for keeping
families together forever, then I can't have a testimony about the
priesthood. It is the priesthood power that gives temple work its
eternal effects. "The priesthood is the eternal power and authority of God. Through the priesthood God created and governs
the heavens and the earth. Through this power He redeems and
exalts His children, bringing to pass 'the immortality and eternal
life of man' (Moses 1:39)."[2] That's why temple marriage is supposedly necessary, because when you're married civilly it's only
till death do you part.

You need the priesthood power to seal your marriage for eternity, not just for life. But if I don't have a testimony about the priesthood, then I can't have a testimony of the Restoration and Joseph Smith. Peter, James, and John supposedly came and gave their priesthood power, which was given to them directly by Jesus, to Joseph Smith. If I don't believe Joseph Smith had the priesthood, then he wasn't a prophet of God and didn't restore Christ's Church.

But I *do* have a testimony of Joseph Smith. I've been to Palmyra and walked through the Sacred Grove. I know Joseph Smith was a prophet called of God. I know God and Jesus Christ came to him in those woods. No, he wasn't perfect. No man or woman, not even the prophets and apostles, are perfect. But I do know that he did what God asked him to do. So if I know that, then why don't I know if the priesthood or temples are true? When I received my patriarchal blessing I knew it was from God. But because I haven't seen the blessings it promised, now I'm not sure if it really was God speaking to me.

I'm still confused and not quite ready to commit. Going to church and reading these quotes makes me happy, but how can I be Mormon when there are these huge fundamental things about the gospel that I don't believe? Being Mormon means you believe in the Book of Mormon, and I can't believe in the Book of Mormon unless I also believe in the priesthood, the Restoration, Joseph Smith, and temples.

Never Again

S and I have been flirting for a few days through texting and Snapchat, and jokingly I tell him if he wants to kiss me then he should just come over and kiss me. Next thing I know, he's at my freaking door. He and I have *never* talked in person before, and now he's at my house to kiss me? I can't even believe he's here right now—this is so awkward. After sitting there as strangers he finally kisses me, but unfortunately, we don't just kiss. After he leaves, I feel beyond disgusting. I immediately regret that decision. He didn't even hesitate, so I just followed his lead. He is a returned missionary, and I just did the unthinkable with him. How could I have let that happen? I fooled around with boys who aren't LDS, but never with a Mormon boy—let alone someone who's endowed! I have no words to describe my guilt and sadness. I feel so horrible, like the worst person on the planet. Obviously I have some respect for the temple, or else I wouldn't feel so guilty about sleeping with someone who's endowed.

I immediately schedule an appointment with the bishop. I know it'll be extremely awkward and embarrassing to tell this bishop (who doesn't even know me) about my latest mistake, but I'm desperate to be clean and rid of the guilt from this horrible thing I've just done, and all the other horrible things I've done over the past nine months. I want to meet with him tonight if possible.

In this moment, I am done with the things of my past. I know it was wrong, all of it. I want NOTHING to do with the horrible things I did and the misery I've felt over the past nine months. It is the worst feeling I've ever felt in my life. Worse than the pain from the heartbreaks, worse than anything I've ever experienced. I don't want to live that life of mistakes anymore. I want to be happy. I want to be clean. And I will do whatever it takes to change and feel the happiness and peace that comes from using Jesus Christ's Atonement to repent. I know now that I need to be Mormon again and commit to the Church. When I've met with the bishop in the past, it was amazing to get that weight off my shoulders and feel peace, so I know this is the only way to receive freedom from the mistakes I've made.

I walk into my bishop's office scared but ready. I know I never ever want to go back to that life I was living. Even though it is hard and embarrassing, I know it's the only way to overcome my mistakes. I've felt how great it is to be clean and temple worthy, and I want that feeling back. All I feel walking out of the meeting with my bishop is overwhelming love. He didn't make me feel like a horrible person or a sinner; he made me feel like a cherished and beloved daughter of God. I don't think my bishop realized what he was getting himself into when we met tonight. I basically word vomited and just spilled everything I've ever done. When I explained to him the things I did while inactive from the Church, he realized these were serious things that would require us to meet more often. Sexual sins are always serious and need a bishop's counsel. Whatever he tells me I need to do, I will do it. At this point, I don't even care about the questions I have about the Church. I know I need to repent and truly come back to the Church to feel better about myself and be happy.

Coincidentally, S is in the elders quorum presidency and is assigned to visit me with a member of the stake presidency. I'm not sure who set this meeting up or why, but the whole reason why S texted me in the first place was to make this appointment. I'm still shocked at how easily he did that with me. He's in the elders quorum presidency, and he acted like what we did was no big deal. They come to visit me just a few days after our huge mistake (talk about awkward!). I am completely honest with the stake president and explain all my doubts and questions about the Church. I tell him how I want to be married in the temple more than anything on earth. How I want the type of family I never had growing up. I want a worthy priesthood holder who will honor me, love me, put me first, love me through my weaknesses and trials, and raise our children in the gospel. I say all of this in front of S, and I don't even care that he hears it. I hope it makes him want to repent and be worthy of holding his priesthood. I explain how I am so extremely discouraged with my dating experiences, and at this point, I feel so worthless. Why would any worthy LDS man want me after all I've done? Especially after what I did with S. How can I ever be with my family forever?

The stake president doesn't answer all my questions with his words, but the Spirit he speaks with calms my heart and brings me peace. He tells me how much God loves me, and affirms my worth. He tells me how much of a pioneer I am, and the influence I will have on my posterity. I will never forget the feeling I have after meeting with him and the impact he has made on my heart. Hope finally starts to come back to me.

I'm hopeful that S will want to be with me and work through our repentance process together. I spend days writing him a letter, and I even purchase a picture of the temple for him, trying to convey my Christlike love for him and my hope that he would want to repent with me. I know it'll be hard, but I think if we do it together we can support each other and keep each other accountable to staying clean. I invite S over to read the letter and give him the photo. I am so vulnerable, reading my thoughts and feelings to him. I've been praying and putting so much thought into these words. S doesn't entirely reciprocate the feelings I share, but tells me he does feel very strongly as well. I'm hoping that's a good sign that we'll be able to work things out. I feel so much love for him.

A few days later, I attend the Mesa Temple Easter Pageant with some friends. While we're there, I see S is tagged in very romantic-looking pictures with a girl on Facebook. My stomach drops when I see these photos. I ask a friend of mine if she knows the girl in the pictures, and she does. My friend messages the girl from the photos, asking her if she is dating anyone. As it turns out, the girl replies she has been dating S for a few months—which means he had a girlfriend all while we were talking and when we messed up. I feel horrible for what I've done—I'm the other woman. He cheated on that poor girl with me. Adrenaline shoots through my fingers down to my toes. How could I have been so stupid? He was probably sleeping with her too, and that's why it was like no big deal for him to do it with me. Yuck, I feel disgusting.

My first thought is to call my bishop—by now he's like a second dad to me—but he's working in the Easter Pageant right now. I need to find him while I'm here tonight. I need him to help me work through these feelings because right now I am so devastated. I decide that I am done trying to date, especially S. I can't trust men. I just keep getting lied to and having my heart broken and being used—even by LDS guys. I am DONE. From now on, my only focus is myself. I just started beauty school and this repentance process, so I have plenty to do to keep me busy. I can't allow myself to worry about dating or getting married.

BACK ON TRACK

In one month, my world has turned completely around. God sends me so many signs to help me through this time and guide me back to Him. I receive a text one Saturday in late March from someone I don't know, asking me if I'd like to go to her home to watch the general women's conference with her family. I have no clue who this girl is, and normally I wouldn't want to go hang out with someone I don't know, but for some reason I accept the invitation. The dear stake president who came to my home had told a friend about me, and that friend asked his daughter to send me that text inviting me to their home. I feel the Spirit *so* strongly during that meeting and with that family.

That day, I post the following on Facebook: "John 14:27: 'Not as the world giveth, give I unto you. Let not your heart be troubled, neither let it be afraid.' The Atonement of Jesus Christ and the blessings of the gospel provide so much more happiness than any worldly thing ever could. It is only when I am following the Savior that I truly feel peace and happiness; He calms my troubled heart and fears."³

Over the past few months, I've been seeing my memories on Facebook from one year ago, and each memory is of me bearing such strong testimony of the Atonement and the temple. It is these memories that remind me how happy I was when I was making good choices and had a temple recommend. Even though I was still sad that I hadn't found my husband, I found joy in every day because of the blessings I did have. Especially around this Easter season, these memories remind me of the mercy God extends to me and the power the Atonement can have in my life.

"I know Jesus Christ lives. I know that he died, for me. He did this because he loves his Father, and because he loves me. I know that he suffered so that I don't have to. I know that any trial I go through, he is there, reaching his arms out to help me and guide me. I know that He will forgive me and comfort me through any mistake I make because of his atoning sacrifice for me. I know that following Christ is the way to happiness. He was resurrected and now lives again so that I can rely on him, because he is my Savior, and I love him."⁴

These reminders of how strongly I used to feel and how sure I was in my conviction of the gospel make me realize that it doesn't matter if I don't understand everything about the gospel. What I know to be true *is true*, and that is enough for me.

"I testify that bad days come to an end, that faith always triumphs, and that heavenly promises are always kept."⁵ After months of pure misery, my bad days are finally coming to an end. Hope and joy are returning to me. The faith I'm regaining is trumping my doubts, but we'll have to see on the heavenly promises. Maybe it's still too late for those promises. Even after I repent, I don't know that I'll suddenly be rewarded for making good decisions.

The following general conference weekend is incredible. General conference falls on Easter Sunday this year, and the Saturday session is seriously sent straight from Heaven for me. EVERY SINGLE hymn and talk given could not have been more perfect for me. Even the Easter video shared by the Church is perfect for me. The theme of this video is "Because He Lives," and it explains that Jesus Christ listens to me, that He hears my prayers, that He is walking with me through every step of my life. No matter who I was or who I am, I am not a lost cause. God is clearly trying to tell me He knows me and He knows what I need to hear. Where was this six months ago when I was in such a dark spot? Now I feel like every word spoken at conference is meant for me:

"God cares a lot more about who we are and who we are becoming than about who we once were."[6]

"Today we celebrate the gift of victory over every fall we have ever experienced, every sorrow we have ever known."[7]

"Don't let something you don't fully understand unravel everything you do know."[8]

"He is not waiting to love you until you have overcome your weaknesses and bad habits. He loves you today with a full understanding of your struggles."[9]

"Whoever you are and whatever your past may be, remember this: it is not too late to make that same choice again and follow Him."[10]

I can't even believe how perfect these quotes are. But the small signs don't stop there. A couple days later, Chloe gets married in Utah. I fly up for her wedding, and as I watch her and her new husband exit the temple, it hits me like a ton of bricks: the temple IS true, I can't settle without it, and I *need* to go inside. I need to have faith and know that God has a plan for me, and as long as I do what I'm supposed to, everything else will somehow work out. I cannot let anything distract me from this goal. I will do whatever it takes to get to the temple, whenever that may be.

NOTES

1. Brigham Young, in *Teachings of Presidents of the Church: Brigham Young* (1997), 261–62.
2. "Chapter 13: The Priesthood," *Gospel Principles* (2011), 67–71.
3. Haleigh Everts' Facebook post, March 28, 2015.
4. Haleigh Everts' Facebook post, April 19, 2014.
5. Jeffrey R. Holland, "Lessons from Liberty Jail," Brigham Young University devotional, September 7, 2008; speeches.byu.edu.
6. Dale G. Renlund, "Latter-day Saints Keep on Trying," *Ensign*, May 2015.
7. Jeffrey R. Holland, "Where Justice, Love, and Mercy Meet," *Ensign*, May 2015.
8. Kevin W. Pearson, "Stay by the Tree," *Ensign*, May 2015.
9. Dieter F. Uchtdorf, "Living the Gospel Joyful," *Ensign*, November 2014.
10. Robert D. Hales, "Preserving Agency, Protecting Religious Freedom," *Ensign*, May 2015.

Introducing: My Husband

"Faith precedes the miracle."

—*Spencer W. Kimball*[1]

In addition to focusing on myself, I also try to focus on my new friends and surround myself with the good LDS girls I've been meeting here. No boys, just girls. One of my new LDS friends (the one who confirmed that S had a girlfriend) agrees to go to a Young Single Adult luau with me. I'm really trying to get out of the house, be proactive, and meet more friends who have good standards. I have no intention of talking to any boys, just having fun and meeting new people. I haven't noticed any boys here who I find attractive anyway. I'm just having fun dancing and hanging out with these great new friends. Apparently a boy here sees me, even though I don't notice him, but he adds me on Facebook the next day.

I don't realize I've received the friend request or a message from the boy, CJ, until five days later. It's been a busy week: I just got back from Chloe's wedding in Utah, my dad and stepmom are in town visiting me from New York, I'm busy with school at night, and I still have frequent job interviews. One Friday night I'm randomly looking through Facebook and I notice the message CJ had sent me five days prior: "Thanks for the add, Haleigh. I hope you have a beautiful day." I feel so rude for never reading it, so I promptly respond. I knew someone with his last name, Everts, from my singles ward in Utah, so I think maybe he and I have met before and I just don't remember him. I've also been meeting lots of new people lately from church, so maybe I've just forgotten that I met him. Our conversations are slightly flirty right away. We discuss his mission in New Jersey and my background in New York, beauty school, and sports, but I'm trying to pay attention to my parents during their visit, so I'm not good at responding to CJ's messages. My parents notice my phone making so many noises from the notifications, so they ask who I'm talking to, and I tell them it's a boy who I haven't met yet. Lucky for me, CJ continues to message me, two days in a row, even though I never respond to his last messages.

CJ continues messaging me on Facebook but never asks for my number. I finally ask him if he is ever going to ask me out. I'm not sure why I just asked him that—I'm not interested in dating anyone. I've been turning guys down the past couple weeks, I really don't want to date, nor do I think I should be dating, given my recent past. I guess I'm just annoyed that he's messaging me through the silly Facebook app instead of directly texting me. It's not like I'm even attracted to his pictures—it's just weird that he's messaging me on Facebook over and over again. What does he want? He hasn't asked for my number, hasn't asked me out. What's his purpose? He replies that he does want to ask me out but wants to do it in person. I explain to him that it would be impossible for him to ask me out in person, as we haven't met yet, but that he can ask me out over the phone. He calls me that Sunday night, and with that phone call, my life changes forever.

NOTE

1. Spencer W. Kimball in "Chapter 13: Obedience Born of Faith in God," *Teachings of Presidents of the Church: Spencer W. Kimball* (2006), 135–44.

That Escalated Quickly

"And when we kissed one another for the first time,
I swear I could hear our souls whisper ever
so quietly, 'Welcome home.'"

—Beau Taplin[1]

SACRIFICE TO BE WORTHY

Earlier that day while at church, I felt so strongly about my res-olution to repent and do whatever it takes to get to the temple. I found a quote by President Gordon B. Hinckley that says, "You will come to know that what appears today to be a sacrifice will prove instead to be the greatest investment that you will ever make."[2] That quote speaks to me and motivates me more than ever to do what is necessary to be worthy to enter the temple with a man one day. Even though I had previously given up hope on finding a man to take me there, my hope is renewed in that quote. I don't know how long it will take, but I know I must have a temple marriage as my main focus and do every-thing in my power to be worthy for the day that opportunity comes. I'm not going to go searching for my husband like I used to, but I just want to be worthy and ready for whenever he comes into my life.

Later that Sunday (still before my phone call with CJ), I receive a text from S because he had his disciplinary council with the bishopric. I still care about him, and I'm part of the reason why he got into this mess in the first place, so I wanted to know what was happening. He tells me he's been disfellowshipped, and my heart sinks. "Disfellowshipment is usually temporary, though not necessarily brief. Disfellowshipped persons retain membership in the Church. They are encouraged to attend public Church meetings, but are not entitled to offer public prayers or to give talks. They may not hold a Church position, take the sacrament, vote in the sustaining of Church officers, hold a temple recommend, or exercise the priesthood. They may, however, pay tithes and offerings and continue to wear temple garments if endowed."[3] I feel so horrible that I caused this to happen. Will that be my fate too? I'm worried, but the hope I felt earlier from church today continues within me. I share a post on my Instagram with a picture of the quote from President Hinckley and my thoughts:

"Ask me why I'm Mormon. My answer comes down to this: I'm investing in my happiness and the happiness of the souls I love. Yes, it is a sacrifice. Choosing to be LDS, to follow these 'rules,' and giving up many of the things I might enjoy or find comfortable is all worth it. I've been a member of this church for seven years now, and it hasn't been easy. But I KNOW that it will be worth it. Finding my husband and getting sealed in the temple to him forever is my main goal in life, and I know it will be the greatest investment I'll ever make. I cannot describe the difficulty and heartache I have faced while trying to achieve this goal of mine. But every sacrifice and every tear will be worth it. I have let myself get discouraged too many times, but I always get back up. Sometimes it takes me longer than other times to regain my hope and come back, but I will never stop trying. No matter what trials I face or how discouraged I get, I will never give up on this goal of mine. Because achieving this goal is what will make me the happiest for the rest of my life, and the rest of eternity. It is worth it."[4]

Chemistry with CJ

I tell CJ practically everything about me when we talk on the phone for the first time. We have so much in common! We both love the same movies (Disney especially), music (John Mayer is our fave), and sports (him playing, me watching), and we both have the same views about some controversial/political topics (which is seriously so rare), a passion for families, and a strong desire to have our own families one day. We confide in each other some of the most difficult experiences in our lives. After talking for more than three hours and setting a plan for a date on Thursday after my parents return back to New York, we say goodnight.

The next day, CJ and I start texting immediately, and we can't stop talking. We realize we don't want to wait until Thursday for our date, so we make plans to meet after I'm done with school tonight. I'm at lunch at Chick-Fil-A with parents, and I tell them about this boy who wants to meet me tonight, even though I'm unsure about it. Looking at his Facebook pictures, I don't think he's that cute, and I don't want to date anyone, so why am I bothering to meet him? My dad tells me to meet CJ and not blow it. "Blow it?" I ask. "How could I blow it? He might be a jerk and this might be nothing." But my dad says this boy also could be really special. My dad was right.

After I get home from school on Monday night, CJ comes over. I'm not sure how I could be so dumb—I really shouldn't allow a boy I've only just met to come over late at night to watch Netflix—but CJ proves to not be like any other boy. When I open the door, I'm pleasantly surprised to find him *much* better looking than his Facebook pictures. He's tall, which I love, but quite thin. I'm the heaviest I've ever been in my life and very insecure about my weight, so really thin guys always make me feel even more insecure about my size. But my insecurities soon melt away because our conversation and chemistry is so great. He doesn't try to get frisky with me, even though we're sitting on my bed (which I warned him about—there's no TV in the living room so the only place to watch is in my bedroom). CJ is sweet and just puts his arm around me while we talk and laugh and hardly pay attention to the show.

The next day, my parents ask how things went last night with this new boy. I can't help but smile as I tell them how much fun I had with CJ. Every time I go on a date, my dad asks me when I'll be seeing the guy next. I always thought that was a silly question—boys don't plan second dates with you while you're still on your first date together. But CJ did! He wants to see me again right away, so I tell my dad that I'll be going to CJ's house to watch the NBA playoffs later tonight. J has been texting me recently, and he said he wants to come down to Arizona over Memorial Day weekend to try to fix things with me. I was never going to give him the chance to come back into my life anyway, but now after such an amazing night with CJ, I block J's number because I want to give CJ my full attention.

As excited as I am to see CJ again, I can't help rehashing the conversation I had with S a few days prior about being disfellowshipped. On the first night CJ called me, I told him that I was very recently reactivated in the Church, but he doesn't realize how bad it truly is. That night as we watch the NBA game, we hold hands, and he keeps looking at me, noticing something is wrong (I'm dodging eye contact with him because I'm afraid he'll try to kiss me). I finally explain to him what happened with S and tell him my fear of also being disfellowshipped. I can't believe I'm telling him all this. He's probably going to hate me and think I'm disgusting for all the crap I've done. What good

Mormon boy would want a girl with such a terrible past like mine? This is when I first discover CJ's outstanding level of faith. He assures me that whatever my fate would be, the Lord is in it. CJ shares with me his own experiences with Church discipline and explains how much it has taught him and had a positive effect in his life. I feel much better after discussing everything with CJ, and I am so impressed by his faith and testimony. He isn't judging me—he is sweet and comforting. I never thought Mormon boys could be like this.

Come Wednesday, my parents are about to leave to go back to New York. They've noticed the change in my demeanor—I'm so happy. Before my parents leave for the airport, I tell them how excited I am about this new boy in my life and about our plans to see each other after they leave. They agree that CJ sounds great, and they share their excitement with me. CJ wants to see me as soon as my parents are gone and asks me to come meet him at his school in between classes. I really want to see him too, so I'm willing to drive up. We meet up at the Mesa temple, but the person CJ finds waiting for him is a very sad girl.

I don't know how to feel this afternoon. I'm so excited about the idea of CJ in my life but still so hurt by all the things that happened with R, S, and J that I don't know if I can or should trust CJ. The street name that the Mesa Arizona Temple is on is coincidentally the same as S's last name. Is this a sign, telling me to remember what S did and to not trust CJ? I also don't know if he'll even want me; after all, I'm in a very difficult place in my life. I don't have a temple recommend, nor do I know when I will be able to receive one. My colorful past is so recent, I don't think a good Mormon boy will want someone like me. Even though CJ was so kind to me last night when I told him what I did with S, I'm still afraid he (or any other boy for that matter) won't want me.

When CJ arrives, he hugs me and realizes there are tears in my eyes. I explain to him my deep desire to be inside the temple and how sitting here, outside this beautiful building, just makes me hate myself for ruining that opportunity.

It's the worst feeling to know that the only thing stopping me from going inside the temple is myself and the stupid decisions I made. I see all these people walking out of the temple who just look so happy. I want to have that. CJ looks me in my tear-filled eyes and leans in to kiss me, and fear instantly overcomes me. I place my hand on his chest and stop him from kissing me. I have so many thoughts running through my mind in this moment.

I don't want to kiss anyone without a commitment. I'm done with kissing for fun, and I don't want to risk the temptation to do more than kiss. But do I want a commitment from CJ?

Would CJ want a commitment from me? He doesn't realize what he's getting himself into. My life is a mess!

I've been so hurt by S and J and all the other boys who've just used me, and I don't know if I'm ready to give anyone else a chance and risk getting hurt again. I'm terrified of getting hurt like that again, and I'm so fragile right now.

I apologize to CJ and explain all my thoughts to him. He reassures me that he isn't interested in messing around; he, too, wants a commitment and wouldn't kiss me if he didn't, and he is trustworthy. He promises not to pressure me but to be patient and wait until I'm ready. In the meantime, he will prove himself to me. At first I think, "I've heard that before!" But I take his hand and we start walking around the temple grounds. I notice all the beautiful flowers, and CJ grabs one and places it in my hair. We sit down on a bench under a tree, and as I look at him, I just know I can trust him. I lean in to kiss him. With that kiss, all of the sudden I am overwhelmed with love, and the thought comes to my mind that this might have been my last first kiss.

NOTES

1. Source unknown.
2. Gordon B. Hinckley, "The Question of a Mission," *Ensign*, May 1987.
3. M. Russell Ballard, "A Chance to Start Over," *Ensign*, September 1990.
4. Haleigh Everts' Facebook post, April 19, 2015.

High on the Mountain Top

"I believe that the most important single thing that any Latter-day Saint ever does in this world is to marry the right person, in the right place, by the right authority."

—*Bruce R. McConkie*[1]

WHEN YOU KNOW, YOU KNOW

I might be crazy for thinking that this is my last first kiss. I just rejected CJ not five minutes ago, and now I feel like I love him and will marry him? I don't have a good track record with judging guys. I thought other guys might have been the one. But something seems different about this. The whole way this began is different. I didn't expect anything when CJ messaged me on Facebook. There was no pressure for me to impress him. My mind hasn't been consumed by him, hoping and waiting for him to message me; in fact, he's been the one pursuing me. He isn't trying *too* hard, but he also isn't playing any games. He doesn't act like all the other guys I talked to, and it was intriguing to me at first. I wanted to figure him out; not because he was mysterious, but because I could just tell he was different from the other guys. After all the deep conversations we've had in a mere three days, we really have all the big stuff in common (besides how we cook our steak, which was almost a deal-breaker for him, apparently!). On our first date he had every opportunity to try to make out or who knows what else with me, like so many other guys did. We were watching Netflix, after all! But he was so respectful. He hasn't kissed me until just now, day three! And even after I rejected him at first, he still wants to be with me.

Later tonight after the temple when I'm home from school, CJ and I are hanging out at my house when out of the blue he tells me he loves me! We're literally just sitting there watching a show, and out of nowhere he says, "I love you," as if he's said it to me a million times before. I swear it's like he can read my mind. I just felt the same feeling earlier today! With that exchange of words, we both know we are getting married.

I couldn't have possibly dreamed up a better man for me. The only obstacle we have to overcome is waiting for the temple. I'm terrified I'll be disfellowshipped and we'll have to wait at least a year to be married. CJ says he's willing to wait and we shouldn't get married civilly. We'll see what happens in my disciplinary council. I'm trying to have faith like CJ and believe that whatever happens is for the best, but waiting one year would be horrible! Not to mention extremely risky (if you know what I mean). But I am determined to get to the temple, no matter what.

THE DISCIPLINARY COUNCIL

When the day for my disciplinary council finally comes, I try harder than ever to have the Spirit with me to comfort me. I've been watching Church videos and reading scriptures and praying all day. It's humiliating to go over every little detail about the horrible things I did. Not only do I have to tell my bishop, but also the three other men in the room. Gosh, this is awful—I can't even believe the things I'm saying. Those things I was doing, that life I was living, that is SO not me! I hope they can see that I'm not that person anymore. My heart has completely changed, and I never really wanted to be living that way in the first place. What's even worse than reliving all those horrible decisions is the waiting. As I sit in the hallway waiting for my bishopric to reach a consensus about my discipline, I pray harder than I've ever prayed in my life. I pray for comfort and peace with whatever the verdict is, I pray that God will allow them to know how truly repentant I am and how deep my desire to go to the temple and marry CJ is, and I pray in gratitude for the ability I have to repent and change through Christ's Atonement.

When I'm called back into the bishop's office to hear their decision, I'm open to whatever they have to say. I'm scared, but I'm just ready to move on with my life and work toward the temple, whether that be now or one year from now. The bishop explains to me how this process works, using the Church handbook for guidance, but mostly relying on revelation from the Lord to make their decision. He tells me given the things he's learned about me, the Spirit he feels, and the revelation they received, I will be put on a probation for a period of six months, after which I will be considered for a temple recommend. I can't believe this. I feel so grateful that God knows what I need and was able to communicate that with my bishopric. Most people probably would have received a one-year probation or been disfellowshipped because of the things I did, but this isn't a cookie-cutter or one-size-fits-all thing. Each individual person, circumstance, and situation is different, and it is through the Spirit that each decision is made. I can't wait to tell CJ we can get married in six months!

A Testimony of Timing

I feel like I'm living a fairytale. CJ is so perfect for me, it's unbelievable! It's crazy that after everything I've been through, this is what was waiting for me all along. I know there's no such thing as soul mates, but it is obvious now that God had a plan for me and CJ to come together.

CJ grew up in Southern California, moved to Arizona, then to Utah, and then back to Arizona before he went on his mission a little later than most boys do. We weren't in Utah at the same time, thankfully—he was on his mission at the time I was at BYU. He went to New Jersey on his mission, only a few hours away from where I grew up, so he's experienced the East Coast and is able to understand parts of my New Yorker personality. Not only did CJ want to return back to Arizona when he came home from his mission, but his sister, brother, and parents had all moved here as well. He has experienced difficult trials and heartache like me—he was convinced he was going to marry his girlfriend he left behind, only to be "Dear John-ed" on his mission.

His family has had really difficult trials; CJ's sister was horrifically murdered, but his faith never wavered through that experience. He went through a phase before his mission when he didn't have a strong testimony and had to face church disciplinary action for some bad decisions, so that's why he doesn't judge me for my past. All these things prepared him so well for me.

It's amazing how I always felt the desire to move to Arizona and somehow CJ and I both randomly (or not so randomly) end up here, things didn't work out with J (or R, or anyone else for that matter), which allowed me to move here, and CJ and I both went to that YSA luau. I technically shouldn't have even gone to that luau because it was only for the Mesa stake (I was in the Gilbert stake). CJ had *just* gotten off a plane from a volleyball national tournament game with his volleyball team (which they unexpectedly lost to a number eight team after being ranked second in the country), allowing him to go to the luau on time. He even had an injured ankle I don't understand why he went to the luau when he was on crutches! If they had won the tournament, he wouldn't have been at the luau and seen me there and recognized my Facebook picture the next day. It's all just so perfect, how and when it happened. It's the way it was supposed to be.

I know I wouldn't have been ready to meet CJ at any other point in my life. I had to go through those horrible experiences to prepare myself for him. I couldn't see it at the time; I had no clue what God was doing. It seemed like I was being put through hell, with no light at the end of the tunnel. I honestly didn't think I would EVER get married in the temple. As much as I had wanted an eternal marriage, I was convinced I'd have to settle without the temple. It seemed like God had given up on me because of my bad decisions. I knew that He loved me, but I didn't see or feel Him in my life. Either my patriarchal blessing was wrong, or God was punishing me and took away my chance to have those blessings that I wanted so badly.

If I'd known this is what was waiting for me, if only I'd just had faith and trusted my patriarchal blessing and trusted that God was there for me and had a plan for me, I could have avoided so much misery. But I know it needed to happen. I know I needed to go through every heartache, every disappointment, every doubt, and every question. At one point in my life, I would have asked why a loving Father in Heaven would put me through so much torture or allow awful things to happen to me, even when I was trying to do the right thing. I now know that it doesn't make God happy to see us suffering; He hates it. But He is our parent, and as such, He knows us better than anyone else, He knows what's best for us, and He loves us enough to allow us to experience pain that will eventually lead to a much greater joy. He did it with our Savior and the Atonement, and He does it with us. His commandments aren't meant to make us miserable or hold us back; they're meant to help us learn to act in faith and safely return back to Him, where we can receive eternal joy.

God knows me better than I know myself. He knows how stubborn I am. He knows that I wouldn't have been able to walk away from my previous relationships on my own, so He had the boys end each relationship so that I could be free to move on to the next phase in my life. Both R and J felt the same way—they each felt like they needed to let me go so I could live the life I was meant to live. I thought it was such crap at the time, just a stupid excuse! But now it is clear to me that God was guiding them. I believe he even guided my dad when he said those hurtful things to me when I was trying to drive back to New York. My dad said the only words he could that would have stopped me from going home. Of course we all have agency; it's not like God forced their hands. But He does put the exact things in our path that He knows will influence our decisions.

Yes, hearing those hurtful words from the people I loved was devastating for me, but it's what needed to happen in order for me to learn and change and grow my testimony so that I could be lead here, to this point. God even put those tornadoes in my path to prevent me from moving back to New York. I had to go through all those bad dating experiences to help me see clearly when the right guy came along (a genuinely nice guy—they don't always finish last!). I had to get to the point where I wasn't even worried about dating or getting married, a point where I had complete trust and faith in the Lord and leaned on Him. I am so grateful for His wisdom and His plan. It is *so* much wiser and better than our own!

Engaged (At LONG Last!)

I've shown CJ pictures of engagement rings that I like, and I know he's picked one out for me, but I have no idea what he's chosen or when he's going to propose. It's a Saturday night, I just got off work, and CJ tells me we're going on a double date. Obviously tonight isn't the night. It's 9:00 p.m. when CJ tells our friends we have to be going, because we're going on a hike. Excuse me? A hike this late at night? Maybe he's proposing after all! But as we drive over and hike up to the top of the mountain, he asks me these deep questions about my testimony, and it makes me wonder if he's trying to get to know me better because he's second-guessing our relationship. He tells me he used to come up here to think when he was having a hard time. I ask him if he's struggling with something, but he says no. He's scaring me! Is he actually breaking up with me? He explains to me how mountains are symbolic of temples in the scriptures and how being on a mountain top is like being closer to God. I can't even look at him because I'm shaking and so nervous and excited. Why is he telling me this?

But finally—*finally*—six weeks after meeting, CJ gets down on one knee and asks me to marry him for eternity. We are officially engaged, and I have the ring to prove it! My dream ring! I was terrified to look at the ring at first in case I didn't like it, but wow, is it beautiful. And this time I didn't have to buy it myself. CJ asks me if I'm ready to help him prepare to meet God, and wholeheartedly, I can honestly say yes, yes I am.

I'm so excited to finally, officially be engaged to the man of my dreams, and I can get married in the place of my dreams too! My friends are so happy for me. They saw everything I went through with R and J. They saw me hit the lowest of lows. But now I'm the happiest I've ever been. My dad is really happy for me too, even though he's never met CJ. It's so funny that when

CJ and I first met, my parents were here visiting, and they could have met! My dad says he believes I'm marrying the right guy because I've never called home to complain about CJ. Usually my dad is the person I go to for advice, but I've never had to ask him for help in my relationship with CJ.

My dad's only fear is that I'll change my mind about the Church again, and then CJ won't want to be with me anymore. But that'll never happen again. I could never go back down that road after experiencing and learning and feeling everything I have. He just doesn't understand how I feel about the gospel, but it's fine. My life is so different now than it was even just a few months ago. It's weird that my new life is on the other side of the country, so far away from my whole family. They won't be coming out for the wedding, as they wouldn't be able to view the ceremony anyway, and it's so expensive to come out just for a wedding reception. I totally understand—they have kids in school and it'd be way too much trouble to bring everyone out here. I honestly wouldn't even care if it was just me and CJ that day. I just can't wait to marry him for eternity!

Note

1. Bruce R. McConkie, "Agency or Inspiration—Which?" Brigham Young University devotional, February 27, 1973; speeches.byu.edu.

By Study and Faith

*"Living and maintaining temple-worthy lives
will hold together all that really matters."*

—*Quentin L. Cook*[1]

Even though my probation is for a six-month time period from when I first started meeting with my bishop, that doesn't guarantee that I will be able to receive my temple recommend at the end of the time period. CJ and I *have* to make sure we stay clean. The bishop wants to meet with us now that we're officially engaged, and he reminds us to be careful. We take his reminder seriously and make sure we read from the Book of Mormon every night and study other books about the Atonement. We pray together, we go to church together—it's everything I wanted. CJ is so strong, I am amazed at his willpower. He is determined for us to stay good and never have to meet with the bishop about any slip-ups. I can't believe I scored such an amazing guy to be my husband! He has so much faith, and I'm learning so much from him.

HAPPINESS IN HEAVEN

As we study the scriptures and as I attend temple prep classes to prepare to receive my endowment and be sealed in the temple, I finally understand and get the answers to the questions I've had for so long. In Mormon chapter 9, I learn why it makes sense for me to be separated in heaven from my family if they never accept the gospel in this life or the next:

1   And now, I speak also concerning **those who do not believe in Christ.**

2   Behold, will ye believe in the day of your visitation—behold, when the Lord shall come, yea, even that great day when the earth shall be rolled together as a scroll, and the elements shall melt with fervent heat, yea, **in that great day when ye shall be brought to stand before the Lamb of God—then will ye say that there is no God?**

3   Then will ye longer deny the Christ, or can ye behold the Lamb of God? Do ye suppose that ye shall dwell with him under a consciousness of your guilt? **Do ye suppose that ye could be happy to dwell with that holy Being, when your souls are racked with a consciousness of guilt that ye have ever abused his laws?**

4   Behold, I say unto you that **ye would be more miserable to dwell with a holy and just God, under a consciousness of your filthiness before him, than ye would to dwell with the damned souls in hell.**

5   For behold, **when ye shall be brought to see your nakedness before God, and also the glory of God, and the holiness of Jesus Christ, it will kindle a flame of unquenchable fire upon you.**

I can't be selfish and wish for my family members to be in a place where they wouldn't be comfortable. In order for them to be comfortable and happy, they need to dwell in whatever place is best suited for them. If they're not prepared to return to God's presence, they won't be happy with God, they'd be happier without Him in a lesser degree of glory.We each have to go where we'll be happiest, and that won't be the same place for everyone, so I need to be patient with their journey of progression. Imagine getting invited to the most extravagant party, but the whole time feeling like you don't belong or fit in there. No matter how amazing the party is, you wouldn't be able to enjoy it. This is the whole reason for having all the different kingdoms in heaven—it makes complete sense to me now. God isn't being mean and separating us from each other; He loves us enough to sacrifice being with us if that's what will make us happiest.

Celestial Marriage

I always knew marriage was important, but I didn't realize how important *temple* marriage was until I actually started preparing to receive my endowment. In Matthew 19, I learned how critical commitment is, especially in a temple marriage:

5 And said, For this cause shall a man leave father and mother, and shall **cleave to his wife: and they twain shall be one flesh**?

6 Wherefore they are no more twain, but one flesh. **What therefore God hath joined together, let not man put asunder.**

While my parents and my future children are, of course, so important, and I love them and the ideal situation would allow us all to be together forever, it is the bond between husband and wife that matters most. Husbands and wives become one flesh, with one united purpose: to live with our Heavenly Parents and eventually become like Them. And only the temple sealing can provide that bond that ties us forever as one. In Doctrine and Covenants 131, I learn more about *celestial* marriage.

1 In the celestial glory there are three heavens or degrees;

2 And **in order to obtain the highest, a man must enter into this order of the priesthood [meaning the new and everlasting covenant of marriage]**;

3 And if he does not, he cannot obtain it.

4 He may enter into the other, but that is the end of his kingdom; he cannot have an increase.

In order for us to become like our Heavenly Parents and live with Them in the highest level of the celestial kingdom, we need to be sealed for eternity in the temple in this life or the next. It is the marriage relationship that matters more so than any other relationship. A temple marriage is not something worth sacrificing; on the contrary, it is the one thing worth sacrificing anything and everything else for. Even though the goal is to have all our loved ones together, I now understand that those other relationships aren't as important as an eternal marriage. It sounds harsh, but I have faith that we will all end up in the places where we will receive the most happiness, even if that means we aren't all together. Before I started studying these topics, I didn't need to know all the answers; I had enough faith to get by without knowing. But I feel stronger somehow, now that I have a better understanding of these gospel principles.

BATTLING INSECURITIES

Even though I have all the answers to my questions and I am so happy with CJ, I still feel a lot of guilt and insecurity. But CJ teaches me so much and helps me become a better version of myself. He helps me to learn more about the Word of Wisdom and the sacredness of our bodies. I finally start living a healthy lifestyle, and I feel so much better about the way I look and the way I view myself, now that I'm losing weight. But even though I'm more confident in my appearance, I feel like I don't deserve CJ, and I can't understand why he wants someone who's made so many terrible mistakes. He was so in love with his ex-girlfriend who Dear-John-ed him. I know she was his perfect type, and I'm really not. If he had to choose between the two of us, would he still pick me? He's great at communicating how much he loves and appreciates me, but I can't help but feel like he should want someone else, that he deserves someone else, someone who hasn't done the things I've done. Someone who is already healthy and thin—unlike me, as I'm only now learning how to take care of my body just because of the things CJ has taught me. I know we're meant to be, but I can't get over how much I hate myself for the things I've done and the insecurities I feel. Why does he want me? For a time I felt like I didn't have any good qualities, that I was a worthless nothing. But CJ, who is SO extremely smart, is talented in a million different ways, has incredibly strong faith, is wonderfully silly and sweet, so good looking and so loving—he sees enough good in me that he wants to be with me FOREVER!

I hate myself for putting us in this position of having to wait to get married. Finding CJ is such a miracle and he's just so perfect for me. How is it possible that he loves me back as much as I love him (which has never happened because I've always been way more into the guy than he was into me) and he wants to be with me forever? FOREVER! That's the biggest commitment ever! He could have any good Mormon girl, and yet he wants me? Someone who was so horrible? I know when things are repented of they're gone and wiped clean, but that doesn't mean I forget what I did. I'm always open with CJ and tell him about all my guilt and insecurities, and he reminds me of something. Who is it that wants me to be unhappy and stuck in my past sins and feel like I'm not good enough? Those feelings don't come from God. I am different now; practically everything about me has improved and changed for the better. Part of repentance and conversion is having a change of heart, which I totally have had. I'm not that same person anymore. CJ isn't marrying who I used to be; he chose me for who I am now and who we can become together. Now that I've changed, drawn closer to God, and applied the Atonement in my life, I deserve my happily ever after with him.

Note

1. Quentin L. Cook, "Shipshape and Bristol Fashion: Be Temple Worthy—In Good Times and Bad Times," *Ensign*, November 2015.

For Time and All Eternity

"Celestial marriage brings greater possibilities for happiness than does any other relationship."

—*Russell M. Nelson*[1]

The Temple at Last

I'm finally released from my probation! To celebrate, CJ and I go to the temple together for the first time to do baptisms for the dead. It's October 2, CJ's birthday. I can't describe how full my heart is as I walk into the beautiful Gilbert temple and hand the worker my recommend. It feels amazing. I deserve to be here. I answered each question in that recommend interview honestly, and I know I am worthy to enter this sacred building. And I'm here with my soon-to-be husband. One day, we will come to the temple with our children so they can do baptisms for the dead too. I am so full of gratitude for the ability I have to be here. The Atonement is the greatest gift. I would have nothing if it weren't for Christ's sacrifice for me. CJ and I both have made our fair share of mistakes in our lives and spent some time not living the type of life Christ would want. At one point, we didn't even know if we truly believed in Him or what it meant to be a disciple of Christ. It took some time before we came unto Christ and really took His name upon ourselves. But when we did, everything in our lives changed.

When I left the Church, I forgot all that Christ had done for me. I didn't keep my faith that was once so strong. But when I finally regained my faith and acted in that faith to use Christ's Atonement, my life became so much happier. My regained faith in Christ led me to my bishop's office to repent. If it weren't for Christ, I wouldn't have ever had the opportunity to overcome my past. I wouldn't have been able to get over the things that have broken my heart. I wouldn't have been able to become worthy to go to the temple and be with my family forever. I am here because of Jesus Christ.

My endowment is scheduled for the ninth and our sealing on the sixteenth. As my endowment day approaches, I'm so excited but also so nervous. So many people leave the Church after they receive their endowments because they think the temple ceremony is weird or scary. I've heard horrible things about it, and I have no idea what to expect. This is a huge deal for me. I've wanted this for so long, especially now that my faith is stronger than ever. I've been preparing for months, I know I'm ready.

My mother wants to fly out for my endowment ceremony, but I know it would be a distraction from the Spirit. We haven't had a good relationship for a long time, and recently, it's gotten much worse. I'm not ready to have her with me, especially on the day when I need to be close to the Spirit. I'm not getting endowed just so I can get married. This isn't just a check mark on a list for me. I want to learn more about God and become more like Him. I want to take whatever necessary steps to bring me closer to eternity. It is entirely about me, and I want it to be perfect without any distractions.

Leaving the temple this special day, I feel like a completely different person. I feel empowered and motivated to go forward and conquer any challenge that comes my way. I feel so loved and special. I feel unbelievably forgiven and clean. All the guilt I still felt, all the insecurities I felt—they're all gone now. I love garments; they feel so comforting. I love all the new things I've learned. I love the temple. It isn't scary or weird—it is so enlightening and happy! I am so grateful for all those who helped me get finally here. It was heartwarming to see so many people who love and support me there to celebrate this step in my life. It's a special feeling I will never forget. I wouldn't be here if it wasn't for them, all those sweet people there to welcome me.

God has a plan, and these people are part of that plan for me. He has created a way for us to receive this happiness and come closer to Him. The plan is laid out perfectly clear. He gave us Christ to learn from in the scriptures. He gave us prophets and apostles to speak to us several times a year so we can be guided through our modern day. He gave us prayer so we can receive personal revelation and have our questions answered. He gave us the Holy Ghost to guide and comfort us. Everything we need, we have. This is where He wants us to end up, and He's shown us how. We can't be stubborn or impatient or prideful and try to make our own imperfect plans happen. We need to be humble so we can learn and grow and allow God to teach us what He has planned for us. We need to be patient because God's plan and timing is much wiser than our own. We need to be cooperative and just do what God has asked of us because He is our Father, He knows best, and following Him is the only way to get here. What a special place the temple is; I had no idea how wonderful it would be.

Worth Waiting a Thousand Years For

Our wedding planning was done so quickly, and now the day is finally here! My parents have been amazingly supportive and gracious, even though they can't come into the temple. I offered to do a ring ceremony so my dad could walk me down the aisle and our non-temple-recommend-holding family members could attend and see us exchange rings and vows, but my dad said he didn't care about the ceremony and didn't want me to go through that extra trouble for him. He just cares about me marrying the right guy. My dad doesn't like the Mormon Church, but I am so grateful he isn't making this special day about him or starting a fight about the Church. Instead, he's just giving me love and support. My mother attends the sealing, but she and I still struggle to get along throughout the whole day.

Our wedding isn't a traditional Mormon wedding per-se, because most of my family isn't here or able to enter the temple, and neither can some of CJ's family members. Some people might not understand my choices for our wedding, but I'm just doing what I know I personally need to do in order to have the greatest, happiest, most sacred and spiritual experiences possible today.

This is the day I've dreamed of and longed for SO LONG. This is the day I always wanted more than anything and thought I'd never have. I went through so much to get here. I worked so hard to make my way back to be worthy to enter this temple. This is the day when all my dreams come true. I suppose some people's feelings are hurt by this, but today is about me and CJ, and no one and nothing can distract me from the day that I finally start my forever family. This is the happiest day of my life.

Note

1. Russell M. Nelson, "Celestial Marriage," *Ensign*, November 2008.

Real Life

*"A happy and successful marriage
depends on two good forgivers."*

—*Lynn G. Robbins*[1]

From One to Two to Three

I am now married to my soulmate. We became soulmates the moment we promised ourselves to each other and to God. Our sealing was so beautiful; we both bawled our eyes out because we were so moved by the Spirit. Now we get to live happily ever after! I feel like I have everything I always wanted.

We are blessed to be able to get pregnant right away. Originally, I wanted to wait two years to have a baby because I knew we'd be moving away for CJ to go to chiropractic school. I just wanted to enjoy our time as newlyweds and get accustomed to CJ's school and the Pacific Northwest before we started having babies and making life more challenging. But when CJ and I discuss having babies, I feel like I'm hit by a train with an undeniable prompting to have a baby right away. CJ agrees to follow the prompting, and as quickly as we decide to try, we are pregnant. I pray so hard for this baby—I know we need her.

I start a new job shortly after finding out I'm pregnant, and I work extremely long days. CJ is still finishing his undergrad in nutrition while also working two jobs. I'm exhausted when I get home every night—pregnancy drains all the energy I have—so I fall asleep much earlier than CJ does. We hardly see each other, but we're still living in newlywed bliss, even though our time together is short. I experiment with making healthy meals, we enjoy the excitement of this little girl growing inside me, and we love being our own little family as we celebrate the holidays together. I think our life is pretty dang perfect, but it isn't long after the happily ever after starts that a villain attacks.

A Bump in the Road

During the first few months of our marriage, I admire and respect and look up to CJ in every way possible. I put him on such a high pedestal—in my eyes he is perfect. Us finding each other has been the biggest miracle of my life. Marrying him is the happiest day of my life. People say the first year of marriage is the hardest, but I don't see that at all. I'm in newlywed bliss—at least until eight months in. Then with this pregnancy and my job and CJ's schooling and his jobs and some trials that pop up, I start having a really hard time in my marriage. It takes me a while to realize what's been going on and why things have gotten so bad. I'm at the point where I honestly feel like I don't like my husband because of the trials that have come up, I don't want to be around him, and I'm not happy in my marriage. It kills me just to think about it. I ADORE CJ, and I mean *adore*. So how on earth did my feelings change so much, and so quickly?

During this period of struggle, I give birth at home to our perfect, sweet angel girl, Ireland. And everything changes when that baby girl is born. I've always been on the defense of my marriage; because of the things I studied at BYU, I know that you have to always protect your marriage. But now that we have Ireland, I'm extremely defensive and protective of my family. I can tell that Satan is trying to destroy my family (as he always does when good things are happening). How dare he try to ruin the family that means everything to me and that I want more than anything! Well, I'm not going to let that happen. I am more determined than ever to overcome the fiery darts being thrown at my family and make us resilient. But in reality, I'm trying to make us perfect.

I take everything I learned at BYU studying marriage and families and go into overdrive. I'm basically trying to change everything we do in our family. We don't pay attention to each other anymore. I pay attention to Ireland all day long, and I'm upset because it seems like CJ doesn't want to play with his newborn baby who he doesn't get to see all day. We don't do anything spiritual on Sundays (besides going to church) to help keep the Sabbath day holy. We don't really spend time together as a family—sitting next to each other on the couch while we watch TV or look at our phones isn't quality time. We never do anything fun. Our date nights aren't centered around bringing us together as a couple or spending quality time together, just eating food. I am so done with this way of living. This is NOT what I envisioned for my family.

I try to make changes, but I just end up complaining about everything in my life, all the time. CJ is working three jobs and is in the last semester of his undergrad right now. He works so hard for our family, and after a long day he wants to relax, but I'm being selfish and only look at what he isn't doing instead of all the things he does for us.

A Dark Place

Things have gotten harder since we've moved to Washington for chiropractic school. It's a huge adjustment for me. I feel so alone and sad. Almost instantly, my entire life has changed. We don't have any money to buy anything because we are living off loans and have no income. I feel trapped, with no one to see and nowhere to go. I miss my new family and friends in Arizona. I miss the warm sunshine. I'm alone all day with Ireland, and then when CJ gets home, he goes straight to studying—for *hours*. He's never around, physically or mentally. So I complain some more. I complain about not being able to buy anything or go out to eat because we don't have money, about how horrible the weather is in Washington, how I don't fit in with anyone here, how I don't have friends, how boring it is to just be a human cow to our newborn without any adult interaction, etc. I complain about everything. I put all the blame on CJ for these miserable things in my life.

There have been a few occasions over the past few months when I've considered walking out the door and ending our marriage. Of course that's not what I want, but I don't see how things can get better. I'm still so hurt by the mistakes that were made in the beginning of our marriage—CJ really upset me, and I don't like the way he's been treating us lately. I live in fear every day that he won't change and I will just keep getting hurt. I'm sick of us bickering all the time and feeling so unhappy. I can't live in a house and share everything with someone I can't trust. I don't want my daughter to be raised in a home with so much negativity and without the Spirit. I pray so hard to be able to forgive CJ and just move on. He's repented of his mistakes and asked for my forgiveness, so why can't I forgive him? I've met with my bishop about it and it's helped a little, but I can't seem to let it go fully. I don't want to remember the things that hurt me so badly, but I can't stop replaying them in my mind—it keeps popping up. I can't get over my fear that I'll have to relive this pain for the rest of my life.

I know I need to talk to CJ about what I've been feeling. I tell him I'm not happy in our marriage and I don't like him anymore. I don't like the way we interact, I don't like the things he's done, and I don't see him the same way I used to.

But I didn't realize how all my complaining has been affecting him. I didn't realize that he doesn't really like me either right now, because I have been miserable to be around. I'm not silly or playful or happy or affectionate anymore. I'm not nice or loving. I haven't been doing anything thoughtful or considerate like I used to. When we first got married, my world revolved around CJ; I was always trying to make him happy and do nice things for him. But now all I've been doing is thinking about myself and all the things I *don't* have. I'm grumpy and mean all the time. I put all the blame on my sweet husband and criticize everything he does. Yes, he is doing things that are wrong too, but it's hard for him to be nice to me when I'm being awful to him. I haven't been looking inward and trying to change myself, I'm trying to change everything else around me. But never once has CJ complained about me. He calls me out when I'm being mean to him but always forgives me and never holds it against me. But I haven't forgiven him for things he did that hurt me. I let it build up and then I add a bunch of other stuff on top too. I don't look for the good in him. I don't try to love him better. I just try to change him and change our life.

I don't have faith that CJ really can change for good and won't hurt me like that again. Yes, he's repented, but that doesn't mean he's suddenly perfect and won't ever make those same mistakes again. I don't have faith that God will help us both to change; I feel like it's up to us to change on our own, but it isn't working. We're not getting better, even after all the talks we've had. But to be fair, I'm not really doing anything to help the situation, either.

I'm not doing things to invite the Spirit into our home, and we aren't attending the temple or saying prayers together. How could God help us change if we aren't doing the things He's told us will change our hearts?

I feel miserable every day—the only thing that brings me joy is my sunshine baby girl. I realize now why I felt the prompting so strongly to get pregnant right away, and it's because I *need* this baby. Without her, I don't think I would still be here willing to stay and work on my marriage. I'm so discouraged and afraid, but Ireland gives me enough joy and motivation to keep me hanging on to my family.

After many hours of discussing everything with CJ, we both agree we need to make some changes. I need to complain less, be more positive, and try harder to forgive. He needs to think before he speaks, be quick to admit when he's wrong, and apologize. And we both need to read our scriptures together and pray every day. We need the strength that the Book of Mormon provides to resist temptation and feel the Spirit. Neither of us are perfect, and we both need to make an effort to do better.

But all I want is for my family to be perfect. I see women on social media who have seemingly perfect lives—a beautiful home, husbands who always surprise them with gifts or vacations (CJ and I never even went on a honeymoon), the most lovey-dovey photos that depict a perfect marriage, always shopping and wearing the cutest outfits, perfect skin, hair, teeth, etc. I compare my life to the things I see online, and I feel like I have nothing compared to them. I have this picture in my mind of a family so centered on Christ, so different from the one I grew up in.

But after discussing our situation with CJ, I guess I have a wake-up call and realize that regardless of all the things I learned at BYU, regardless of how miraculous it is that CJ and I found each other, regardless of how amazing our baby is, we are not perfect and we never will be in this life. It is completely righteous to desire to be better—that's what we're all here for. But the way we go about it is what matters. Treating my husband like crap and blaming him for our family's imperfections doesn't fix anything. Comparing this short stage of our lives to others' social media lives doesn't motivate me, it depresses me. When things aren't going well, I need to have faith and do my part to help my family in the ways the matter most, in the ways that are truly important.

TIME TO FORGIVE

I want to be able to forgive CJ so badly, but regardless of all my prayers and wishing, I still can't see him in the same light I used to. I still can't stop thinking about the things he did that hurt me. Even though we cleared everything up and are both doing much better, I still have been haunted by the past. It's affecting every part of our marriage. But then I read the First Presidency message for February 2017, and my heart is softened. President Monson says, "If we would keep the commandment to love one another, we must treat each other with compassion and respect, showing our love in day-to-day interactions. Love offers a kind word, a patient response, a selfless act, an understanding ear, a forgiving heart. In all our associations, these and other such acts help make evident the love in our hearts."[2]

There is so much hatred in world today, so much selfishness. This is not ever going to solve any problems! If our hearts and minds are only focused on ourselves, if our hearts are holding grudges and negative thoughts and feelings, there will never be peace in our homes. I thought I was trying hard to forgive CJ, and I really wanted to. But deep down I realize I wasn't trying to forgive him; I was purposely holding onto the pain from what he'd done in order to protect myself in case he did something again; it couldn't hurt me if I was already hurting from the last time.

President Kimball said, "The essence of the miracle of forgiveness is that it brings peace to the previously anxious, restless, frustrated, perhaps tormented soul. In a world of turmoil and contention this is indeed a priceless gift."[3] That is me! That is exactly how I feel—anxious, frustrated, restless, and tormented. President Monson taught, "Love is the remedy for ailing families, ill communities, and sick nations."[4] If we want to see a change in our homes, our families, our neighborhoods, and our world, we need to show more love. We will all be SO much happier if we were able to forgive and have love. There have been plenty of people, not just CJ, who have done things to hurt me or my family recently. But I don't want to feel anxious, restless, frustrated, or tormented by those hurtful things. I want to be free of that. So I have to forgive and choose to feel love instead. That also means I need to love myself.

Happiness, forgiveness, and love are a choice. I love my family more than anything. We are all imperfect. Hardships inevitably come, even when I think my life is perfect. But if we are quick to forgive and show love in those imperfect moments, we can have peace and happiness in our homes. I need to speak kind words and give compliments instead of criticism. I need to be more patient with others and myself. I need to put myself in someone else's shoes and understand what they might be feeling or thinking, and realize no one has a perfect life. Most of all, I need to purge my heart of negative feelings and forgive. Now that I've finally done these things, I am truly able to forgive CJ and move forward in faith in our marriage. This trial has taught me a great lesson, and now our marriage and family relationships are stronger than ever. There are times when people are so toxic that you do need to unfollow them or distance yourself from them, but that is not the case in my relationship with CJ or in our family.

We both need to humble ourselves, sacrifice, and work hard to draw nearer to each other and to the Savior.

NOTES

1. Lynn G. Robbins, *Love Is a Choice* (Salt Lake City: Deseret Book, 2015).
2. Thomas S. Monson, "'As I Have Loved You,'" *Ensign*, February 2017.
3. Spencer W. Kimball, *The Miracle of Forgiveness* (Salt Lake City: Bookcraft, 1969), 363.
4. Thomas S. Monson, "'As I Have Loved You,'" *Ensign*, February 2017.

To Walk in the Light

"Look unto me in every thought; doubt not, fear not."

—*Doctrine & Covenants 6:36*

My daughter is eleven months old and hasn't been feeling well for the past few days. She just cut her first molar, so I know she's in pain and feverish from that. When I get her from her crib one morning, she immediately falls down. Ireland started walking at nine months, so she shouldn't be falling so easily. But with each step she takes, she falls and struggles to get back up. I look at her legs, feet, and ankles. Her left ankle looks swollen ever so slightly and a little bruised maybe. I send a picture to CJ, and he thinks maybe she got it stuck in her crib rail or something. As the hours go by, her ankle gets more swollen. When CJ comes home we decide we should take her to Urgent Care to get x-rays, just to be safe. We decide we'll eat dinner after we're done at Urgent Care, not realizing we won't be coming home at all.

Urgent care sends us to the ER, and the ER sends us to a children's hospital in Portland. I refuse to go to the children's

136

hospital—this is ridiculous. No one knows what's wrong with her ankle. The x-ray shows nothing, and her blood work just shows inflammation. Yeah, her gums are inflamed; we already knew that. It's after midnight, it's freezing outside, our poor baby has been poked and proded by needles for hours, and everyone's exhausted, not to mention hangry. But CJ says he feels it's important to go just to be safe. He won't ignore a prompting. I begrudgingly go to the children's hospital, but only after we stop and get some food.

We were sent to this hospital because we were told they had a small instrument here to collect fluid from her swollen ankle joint so they could test it and see what's happening. But upon arrival, they tell us they know it's a bone infection and they don't need to run any tests. I'm a wreck. I refuse to believe them. They can't know that just by looking at her ankle. I'm sick of seeing my baby screaming and crying in pain. I try to comfort her, but she's hysterical. They set us up in a room for the night, but CJ and I don't even attempt to sleep until six in the morning. An orthopedic surgeon comes to meet with us around eight that morning, and he tells us he feels very strongly that she needs surgery *now* to remove the infection. How did this happen? My poor baby. She needs to go under anesthesia so that she'll stay still during the MRI. The doctors hope that the MRI will give them a better idea of where in the ankle she's having this problem. When she wakes up I just want to nurse her, but I'm not allowed to since she'll have to go under anesthesia again for the surgery in a few hours. Now my sick baby has to starve too.

We hold and kiss our daughter one more time before she goes back for surgery. I still can't believe this is happening. We thought she sprained her ankle; we thought we'd only be in Urgent Care for a couple hours, and now here we are. As she is wheeled back for surgery, I'm terrified that she'll never wake up from anesthesia. What will I do if that happens? How will I go on and ever be happy again? Of course I know I can see her again one day, but how will I make it through every day of the rest of my life without her? Tragedy can hit at any time. It's never expected. People make horrible decisions. Accidents happen. Ever since Ireland was born, I've been fearful about what could happen to her. When we're in the car, I imagine getting into a horrific accident and hearing my baby screaming in pain, while I am trapped and unable to get to the backseat and help her. When I hear about the evil and sad things happening in the world, the earthquakes and hurricanes and shootings, I wonder what I would do in the face of such difficulty. In the face of this small calamity, I start to get an idea.

The OR gives us a paper with a number so that we can look on a TV screen and see the status of the surgery corresponding with the number. It was supposed to take thirty to forty-five minutes, but we've been waiting for over an hour. The number they gave us never appears on the screen. I have absolutely no idea what is happening to my sweet baby girl. I notice a door in the waiting room, and I tell CJ that they take families into those rooms and share bad news so that no one else in the waiting room has to hear. I've watched plenty of Grey's Anatomy, so I know what I'm talking about.

As the surgeon comes to grab us from the waiting room much later than expected, CJ and I look at each other with panic in our eyes. What is he about to tell us? He doesn't say a word but leads us into the "bad news room." This is it. We're about to hear something awful. After what seems like an eternity, the surgeon finally tells us her surgery went well and she will quickly recover, which she does.

But what if something had gone wrong? What if something horrible would have happened? If there's anything I've learned in my life it is that faith and fear cannot coexist. Because of Jesus Christ, because of the Atonement, because of the Plan of

Salvation, I never need to fear. He is the light, hope, and truth. He is there to cast out the doubts and the darkness. But if I focus on my fears and my doubts, I can't feel the peace that comes from having faith. I'm not the best at having complete faith and not letting my fears take over. It's so hard during such difficult times to remember that God has a wiser plan, and sometimes there are blessings that come from pain and tragedy.

After discussing this entire unexpected experience with CJ, I am so grateful for his outstanding faith. I'm the worrier who always has to go check on Ireland when she's sleeping, but CJ reminds me that she is always being watched over and whatever happens is part of God's plan, and if something is supposed to happen then it will. CJ balances my anxiety out with his calmness so perfectly. I would lose my mind during a tragedy if it weren't for his faith to help cast out my fears.

Sharing Is Caring

*"True conversion occurs as you continue to act upon
the doctrines you know are true and keep the commandments,
day after day, month after month."*

—*Bonnie L. Oscarson*[1]

I've been married for only two years and have just one child right now. I have so much more life to experience. I know more trials will come. I'm not done growing and learning, so the trials (however big or small) will keep coming. Especially as I try to do good by sharing the gospel and my life experiences through blogging, YouTube, social media, and this book, Satan tries to tear it down. I receive hateful comments on my Instagram posts and YouTube videos; I'm told I'm wrong about the Church every single day, that I don't know what I'm talking about, that the Mormon Church makes you hate yourself, that I'm going to hell if I don't leave the Mormon Church. Anti-Mormon websites and YouTube channels write about me and critique everything I say in my videos. I get discouraged by my lack of aesthetically pleasing and professional videos and photos. I feel inferior to the beautiful women who have perfect bodies, flawless skin, hundreds of thousands of followers, and gorgeous homes and photos.

But I know those outward, materialistic, worldly things don't really matter. The experiences I've had have taught me what matters most. I've learned who I am and how to love myself for all the things on the inside, the things the world will never be able to see clearly. But I know who I am, and it doesn't matter what anyone says about me. What matters is that I try my best each and every day and that Heavenly Father knows my heart's desires.

People, even family, tell me I shouldn't be so open and share all my thoughts and beliefs. There is so much opposition, and my imperfections and flaws are always pointed out. I struggle every day to be patient with my daughter and husband, to be humble and non-judgmental, to take care of my body, to say the right things that I hope will help others, do the simple things I've been commanded and have promised to do. My faith isn't perfect. But I've been through too much and I know too much to *not* share my testimony and my experiences with others.

In a world of so much negativity, destruction, fraud, tragedy, immorality, and sadness, I feel I have an obligation to share some light and joy. Social media and the internet are full of fakeness and evil, so I need to add some authentic goodness. I need to talk about the things no one else does, the things everyone inevitably faces and struggles with. I need people who are burdened with doubts, fears, questions, and insecurities to know they are not alone. Though it may seem like everyone else is living such a perfect life, the highlight reel we see from the outside doesn't show what's happening on the inside. I need people to know that no matter what they've done, how far they've strayed, how worthless they feel, or how hard their trials are, they can find happiness. I need people to know there *is* a light at the end of the tunnel. I need people to know that God is their Father and loves them more than they can comprehend. He doesn't abandon us. He doesn't give up on us. Even if we can't see Him, He is there working His miracles. His wisdom and plan are perfect. It doesn't usually line up with what we think is best or what we want when we want it, but it truly is what is best for us.

Faith does not stop bad things from happening. Faith does not make pain go away. Having faith is not rewarded with a trouble-free life. It might seem like I was instantly rewarded with finding my husband after I came back to the Church, but that's not true. My husband isn't a blessing I was given because of my "good behavior"; it was just part of God's timing for me.

When we have faith, we can find joy through the trials and through the pain. Faith is necessary when we have questions, because we might not get all the answers in this life. I left the Church because my faith wasn't strong enough to be satisfied with the answers I did have, even though there were things I still questioned. My faith wasn't strong enough to get me through the trials that are naturally part of this life's growing and learning experiences. I let fear and doubt control me more than faith and hope. But now I know better. Now I have my answers and a stronger faith than ever before, and thankfully I have a husband with faith to help me during my weak moments. Now I have the strength to make it through the challenges I face and the hope for a bright eternity.

NOTE

1. Bonnie L. Oscarson, "Be Ye Converted," *Ensign*, November 2013.

The night CJ and I first talked on the phone, when I
forced him to call me to ask me out.
April 19, 2015.

The night CJ and I first met, and I warned
him about being in my bedroom.
April 20, 2015.

My baptism.
January 26, 2008.

About the Author

Haleigh Everts is a teenage convert to The Church of Jesus Christ of Latter-day Saints from Upstate New York. Coming from a non-member divorced family, she always dreamed of being married in the temple and having her own eternal family one day. She received her bachelor of science in family studies from Brigham Young University in 2014 and has since tried to teach and help strengthen others' testimonies and families through blogging, social media, and YouTube. Haleigh's dreams came true when she married her husband, CJ, in the Gilbert Arizona Temple in October 2015, and they welcomed their first daughter, Ireland, in August 2016.

Scan to visit

www.foreverts.wordpress.com